YOU'LL NEVER LOOK AT THE NEWS THE SAME WAY AGAIN!

OAHU, HAWAII, U.S.A.

IMAGINE SKATEBOARDING IN THE CLOUDS! Skydiver Jürgen Schneider did just that over the shores of the island of Oahu. Schneider and some skydiving pals also jumped with other gear, including surfboards and flippers, masks, and snorkels. One of their biggest challenges, they say, was bringing the equipment back to the ground in one piece!

NATIONAL
GEOGRAPHIC
KiDS

weird but true!

RIPPED FROM THE
HEADLINES

REAL-LIFE STORIES
YOU HAVE TO READ TO
BELIEVE

TABLE OF CONTENTS

INTRODUCTION

If you've ever thought newspapers were boring, get ready to be amazed! *Weird But True!: Ripped From the Headlines* has all the things you expect in a newspaper—world news, sports and science sections, entertainment stories, and more—but with a twist. Everything in these newsy pages is factual, but also offbeat, odd, surprising, bizarre. In other words, weird but true!

Did you know that playing pinball was once considered a crime? Have you heard about the dog that got married in a $6,000 wedding dress? How about the toilet that doubles as a soccer goalie? These are just a few of the fascinating stories from history and today that you'll find in this exciting addition to the Weird But True series.

Weird But True!: Ripped From the Headlines brings some of the strangest events of all

ART AT THE BOTTOM OF THE SEA
PAGE 122

time to one jam-packed book. From glow-in-the dark piglets in China to robot cameras in Kenya, you'll discover astounding headlines from around the world and mind-bending stories that prove truth really is stranger than fiction. Read all about the four-story-tall rubber ducky currently touring the world. Learn about the World War I troops who took a Christmas break to play soccer or the American explorer who ate 36,000-year-old bison meat. It's all here for you to find, along with awesome pictures and more of the insane facts you love.

Covering animals, athletes, space, food, toys, geography, money, weather, and more, the news stories in this book will open your eyes to the world around you.

Whether you're reading about gargantuan spiderwebs, marveling at skyscrapers made of straw, or learning how to make your own Kool-Aid pickles, one thing is certain—you'll never look at the news the same way again!

CHAPTER 1

WACKY
WORLD
HEADLINES

STORMTROOPER TROOPS ACROSS AUSTRALIA, PAGE 16

T RUBBER DUCK TOURS THE WORLD • "LOST"
FFIC HEY, WHAT'S THAT UNDER THE COUCH? •
N INTO TOYS • SWEDEN FORCED TO IMPORT T
OUT OF TRASH! • STORMTROOPER TROOPS
MERMAID MIX-UP •

Giant *Rubber* DUCK

PITTSBURGH, PENNSYLVANIA, U.S.A.

IF A SMALL RUBBER DUCK CAN MAKE BATH TIME A LITTLE MORE FUN, what do you think happened when a giant, 40-foot (12-m)-tall rubber duck bobbed up and down in the Allegheny River in Pittsburgh? *Lots* of fun! The duck was created by Dutch artist Florentijn Hofman, who titled his sculpture—what else?—"Rubber Duck." Other versions of Hofman's bright yellow floating sculpture have gone for swims in Osaka, Japan; Sydney, Australia; São Paulo, Brazil; Amsterdam, Netherlands; Hong Kong, China; and other places!

TOURS THE WORLD

"LOST" DOG POOP GETS SENT HOME

SPECIAL DELIVERY

BRUNETE, SPAIN

A small Spanish town sent a strong (and smelly) message to inconsiderate dog owners: Scoop the poop, or else! During a one-week experiment, undercover volunteers chatted with dog walkers who didn't clean up their dogs' mess. By sneakily learning the dogs' names and breeds, the town looked up the addresses of 147 offenders. The volunteers then wrapped up individual packages of dog droppings and sent them by messenger to the offenders' homes, marked "Lost Property."

NO SHORTS ALLOWED? NO PROBLEM!

WHO MALE TRAIN CONDUCTORS

WHAT PROTESTED THEIR COMPANY'S "NO SHORTS" POLICY BY WEARING SKIRTS TO WORK

WHERE STOCKHOLM, SWEDEN

WHY TEMPERATURES CAN BE SCORCHING IN THE TRAIN CONDUCTORS' CAR, SO THE CONDUCTORS WERE UNCOMFORTABLE IN THEIR UNIFORM LONG PANTS. THEIR FEMALE COUNTERPARTS WERE ALLOWED TO WEAR SKIRTS, SO THE MEN TOOK THAT OPTION FOR THEMSELVES.

OUTCOME THE CONDUCTORS' EMPLOYER CHANGED COMPANY POLICY AND ORDERED NEW SHORTS FOR MALE STAFF AT LAST!

NEWS FEED

>>> **OFFENBURG, GERMANY:** A FRIGHTENED 75-YEAR-OLD WOMAN CALLED POLICE AT 3 A.M. BECAUSE HER DOORBELL KEPT RINGING. POLICE

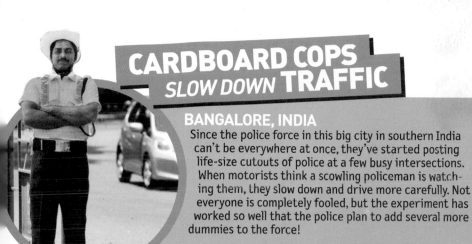

CARDBOARD COPS
SLOW DOWN TRAFFIC

BANGALORE, INDIA
Since the police force in this big city in southern India can't be everywhere at once, they've started posting life-size cutouts of police at a few busy intersections. When motorists think a scowling policeman is watching them, they slow down and drive more carefully. Not everyone is completely fooled, but the experiment has worked so well that the police plan to add several more dummies to the force!

HEY, WHAT'S *THAT* UNDER *THE* COUCH?

PLYMOUTH, ENGLAND
Colin Steer was always curious about a strange dip in the floor under his couch—so curious that, after 25 years of wondering about it, he finally dug down into his home's foundation. What did he find? A medieval well 33 feet (10 m) deep—along with an old sword wedged in its walls! Now a trapdoor covers the well, and the family couch is back in place.

INVESTIGATED AND DISCOVERED THE CULPRIT—A LARGE ANT NEST PRESSING UP AGAINST THE DOORBELL'S SWITCH WIRES.

EVERYTHING OLD IS NEWS AGAIN!

"THINK I'M A SHOE-IN FOR BEST LOOKING TOY?"

WASHED-UP SANDALS TURN INTO TOYS

NAIROBI, KENYA

When marine scientist Julie Church saw baby turtles fighting their way through beach trash to get to the ocean, she knew something had to be done. Taking inspiration from local children who made boats out of old flip-flops, she formed a company, now called Ocean Sole, that turns old rubber sandals from Kenya's beaches into colorful toys!

To make the toys, workers collect the rubber shoes from the shore and wash them thoroughly. Then they glue them together and carve them into giraffes, elephants, warthogs, and other animals. After the finished toys have been washed once again, they're sold in stores all over the world.

IT TAKES ABOUT **FIVE** **TWO-LITER RECYCLED** PLASTIC SODA **BOTTLES** TO MAKE ENOUGH **FIBERFILL** FOR A **SKI JACKET.**

NEWS FEED

>>> ASUNCIÓN, PARAGUAY: A YOUTH ORCHESTRA MAKES MUSIC OUT OF TRASH! KIDS IN THE ORCHESTRA HAVE LEARNED TO PLAY CLASSICAL MUSIC, THE

SWEDEN FORCED TO IMPORT TRASH

STOCKHOLM, SWEDEN

In Sweden, household trash is burned to make energy for heating and electricity. There's just one problem: The Swedes are so good at recycling, they don't make enough garbage to fuel their own power plants!

This unusual situation (which one could say is a very good problem to have) has forced squeaky clean Sweden to buy and import about a million tons (900,000 mT) of trash annually from its European neighbors. That's a whole lot of rubbish!

THE **AVERAGE AMERICAN** CREATES **4.4 POUNDS** (2 KG) OF **TRASH** EVERY DAY.

A-MAZE-ING TRASH!

SÃO PAULO, BRAZIL

Landscape mazes are often created with bushes in a garden, but Brazilian artist Eduardo Srur chose to do something a little different—he built his maze with giant blocks of recyclable trash!

Srur's public art display used up to 110 tons (100 mT) of recyclable waste. The labyrinth he designed covered an area about 4,300 square feet (400 m²). Building blocks were made from compressed plastic bottles, cups, wrappers, paper, aluminum cans, steel cables, and plastic mirrors. The artist's idea was to entertain visitors, while bringing them face-to-face with the massive amounts of household garbage we humans dump out.

IN THE **U.S.,** TWO-THIRDS OF ALL **PAPER PRODUCTS** ARE **RECYCLED.**

BEATLES, AND FRANK SINATRA ON INSTRUMENTS MADE OF OBJECTS RECYCLED FROM A HUGE DUMP NEAR THEIR HOMES. THEY'VE PERFORMED IN BRAZIL, PANAMA, AND COLOMBIA!

STORMTROOPER TROOPS ACROSS AUSTRALIA

A SCUBA REGULATOR CREATED THE SOUND OF **DARTH VADER'S** DIFFICULT BREATHING.

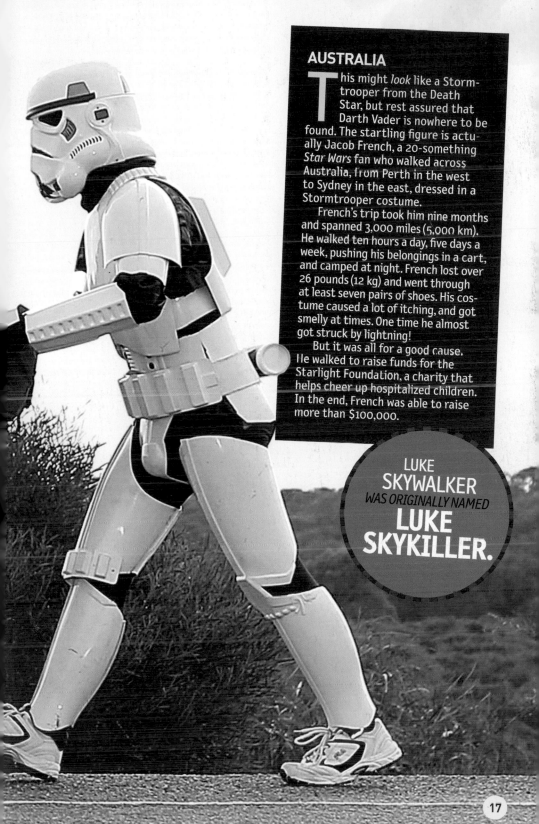

AUSTRALIA

This might *look* like a Stormtrooper from the Death Star, but rest assured that Darth Vader is nowhere to be found. The startling figure is actually Jacob French, a 20-something *Star Wars* fan who walked across Australia, from Perth in the west to Sydney in the east, dressed in a Stormtrooper costume.

French's trip took him nine months and spanned 3,000 miles (5,000 km). He walked ten hours a day, five days a week, pushing his belongings in a cart, and camped at night. French lost over 26 pounds (12 kg) and went through at least seven pairs of shoes. His costume caused a lot of itching, and got smelly at times. One time he almost got struck by lightning!

But it was all for a good cause. He walked to raise funds for the Starlight Foundation, a charity that helps cheer up hospitalized children. In the end, French was able to raise more than $100,000.

LUKE SKYWALKER *WAS ORIGINALLY NAMED* **LUKE SKYKILLER.**

POMPANO BEACH, FLORIDA, U.S.A. ANYONE LOSE AN EYEBALL? WHEN THIS MYSTERIOUS SOFTBALL-SIZE EYEBALL WASHED ASHORE, BEACHCOMBERS WERE STUMPED UNTIL SEA-LIFE EXPERTS FINALLY UNRAVELED THE MYSTERY: IT BELONGED TO A GIANT SWORDFISH.

[SNAZZY SNAPS FROM ALL OVER]

From east to west, from north to south, the world is full of eye-popping sights. See if you can guess what's going on in these pictures—before you read the captions!

TAIZHOU, CHINA *HONK-HONK!* MAKE WAY FOR 5,000 WADDLING DUCKS. A 70-YEAR-OLD FARMER REGULARLY WALKS THESE BIRDS THREE-QUARTERS OF A MILE (1.2 KM) THROUGH TRAFFIC TO A NEARBY FEEDING POND. AND HE NEVER LOSES ANY OF THEM ALONG THE WAY!

DUCKS CAN SLEEP WITH ONE EYE OPEN,
ESPECIALLY WHEN THEY ARE **NEAR THE EDGE OF A GROUP.**

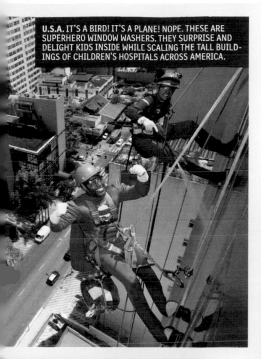

U.S.A. IT'S A BIRD! IT'S A PLANE! NOPE. THESE ARE SUPERHERO WINDOW WASHERS. THEY SURPRISE AND DELIGHT KIDS INSIDE WHILE SCALING THE TALL BUILDINGS OF CHILDREN'S HOSPITALS ACROSS AMERICA.

IT TAKES **3 MONTHS** FOR **WINDOW WASHERS** TO **CLEAN** ALL THE WINDOWS IN THE WORLD'S **TALLEST BUILDING, THE BURJ KHALIFA,** IN DUBAI, UNITED ARAB EMIRATES.

HARBIN, CHINA ASTRIDE A BROOMSTICK, A SWIMMER TAKES A FLYING LEAP OVER A FREEZING COLD RIVER AT AN ANNUAL ICE AND SNOW FESTIVAL. HE'S IN FOR A CHILLY LANDING!

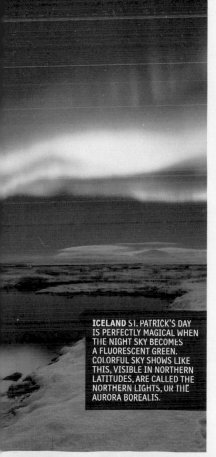

ICELAND ST. PATRICK'S DAY IS PERFECTLY MAGICAL WHEN THE NIGHT SKY BECOMES A FLUORESCENT GREEN. COLORFUL SKY SHOWS LIKE THIS, VISIBLE IN NORTHERN LATITUDES, ARE CALLED THE NORTHERN LIGHTS, OR THE AURORA BOREALIS.

DRESDEN, GERMANY A POLICE DOG NAMED DR. MAX, DISGUISED AS A BABY, DEMONSTRATES AN UNDERCOVER CRIME-BUSTING TECHNIQUE: JUMPING OUT OF A BABY CARRIAGE TO NAB A SUSPECT!

MANATEES SOMETIMES **BODYSURF** WHEN **PLAYING.**

CHRISTOPHER COLUMBUS MERMAID MIX-UP

While sailing in the Caribbean, Christopher Columbus reported seeing three "female forms" that "rose high out of the sea." He described them as mermaids, though he was disappointed that they "were not as beautiful as they are represented." There may be a good reason for that—most historians think he actually saw three manatees!

1493

>>> **MYSTERIOUS ... OR MISUNDERSTOOD?**

1938

RADIO LISTENERS GET REAL SCARE

Millions of Americans listening to a national radio program heard what seemed to be a real news report about aliens landing from Mars and attacking New Jersey and New York. Some panicky Americans actually believed it was true! The host of the show, Orson Welles, told listeners at the beginning of the broadcast, which was called "The War of the Worlds," that the story was made-up. However, many people tuned in too late to hear that announcement, and the story wound up scaring them out of their wits!

DETECTIVE STORY WRITER DUPED

1920

Sir Arthur Conan Doyle, the author of the Sherlock Holmes detective stories, wrote an article "proving" the existence of fairies. He was absolutely serious, and to make his case, he published some photos taken by two young girls showing them playing with fairies in their yard. Turns out that the great detective writer was duped: In 1981 the girls admitted the pictures were fake —the fairies were actually cutouts snipped from a children's book that the girls hung around themselves with hat pins.

LOCH NESS MONSTER MAKES A SPLASH

1933

A London man was driving around Scotland's Loch Ness with his wife when he saw the "nearest approach to a dragon or pre-historic animal that I have ever seen in my life." The creature was apparently walking across the road toward the lake carrying an animal in its mouth. The man's story was published in a local newspaper. That same year, the first photo of the creature also appeared in the newspaper, spurring the excitement around the Loch Ness Monster that still exists today.

UFO SIGHTING: FACT OR FANCY?

1952

A few minutes before midnight on July 19, 1952, an air traffic controller at Washington National Airport saw blips on his radar. At an air force base ten miles (16 km) away, people gaped as bright orange objects circled the sky and then streaked off at blinding speeds. Radar and visual sightings continued, and the next night there were more. After an investigation, the Pentagon dismissed the sightings as "a temperature inversion." But for those who saw them, that explanation was not a satisfactory one.

SUMO WRESTLERS *MAKE BABIES* CRY

TOKYO, JAPAN

Every year, a temple in Tokyo holds a crying-baby contest. In this 400-year-old tradition, sumo wrestlers hold the babies and try to make them cry, by growling or making scary faces. The contest is thought to bring good luck and health to the babies. Each match-up has two babies. Whichever one cries first, or wails the loudest, wins!

SWEDISH TOWN ON WILD GOOSE CHASE

WHO FRUSTRATED TOWN OFFICIALS

WHAT SET UP PLASTIC GERMAN SHEPHERDS TO SCARE AWAY FLOCKS OF CANADA AND BARNACLE GEESE THAT WERE FOULING UP THE TOWN'S PARKS

WHERE SOLLENTUNA, SWEDEN

HOW THE PLASTIC GERMAN SHEPHERDS WERE TWO-DIMENSIONAL CUTOUTS. THEY WERE ATTACHED TO POSTS THAT ALLOWED THEM TO TURN AND SPIN WHEN THE WIND BLEW.

OUTCOME GEESE ARE SUPPOSED TO BE AFRAID OF GERMAN SHEPHERDS, BUT THESE SMART GEESE CAUGHT ON RIGHT AWAY TO THE "GERMAN SHEPHERDS" FLAPPING IN THE BREEZE. IT WASN'T UNTIL A REAL CHIHUAHUA SHOWED UP, ACCORDING TO ONE WITNESS, THAT THE GEESE "GOT THE FRIGHT OF THEIR LIVES."

NEWS FEED

>>> CHICAGO RESIDENT CLINTON SHEPHERD SPENT TWO DAYS ON A FERRIS WHEEL, CIRCLING 384 TIMES BEFORE CLAIMING

BEIJING, CHINA

A doctor built a mountaintop on his apartment building, but officials ordered him to demolish it. Neighbors worried that their building might collapse under the weight. The doctor said he wanted to cover ugly roof pipes and make his penthouse prettier, but he neglected to get permission to build his phony mountaintop first. For six years he transported wood panels and shrubbery upstairs via the freight elevator. The rocks, he said, were fakes.

STEEP TROUBLE FOR URBAN MOUNTAIN MAN

WAGGA WAGGA, AUSTRALIA

Swarms of spiders launched an emergency evacuation to higher ground when a week of heavy rain flooded their underground dwellings. They blanketed vast areas of the city and countryside with massive silk webs that were engineered to give them support as they fled the rising water. Their thick webs looked just like trampolines stretching through the bushes and trees.

SPIDERS BLANKET AUSTRALIAN CITY IN WEBS

THE RECORD FOR THE LONGEST THEME PARK RIDE EVER. SHEPHERD HAD A TV SET IN HIS GONDOLA AND SPENT HIS TIME WATCHING MOVIES AND PLAYING VIDEO GAMES.

BICYCLE

PRAGUE, CZECH REPUBLIC

If you've ever wished you could fly like Harry Potter, this might be your chance—if you'll settle for a flying bicycle instead of a broom!

A team of engineers and designers from the Czech Republic have developed the F-bike, a bicycle that flies like a helicopter. The bike has six propellers—a pair in the front, another pair in the rear, and one on either side of the seat. Each propeller has its own battery-powered engine.

The flying bicycle took a year and a half to make—and the team of inventors was inspired by flying machines in movies and fantasy stories.

The pictures shown are from a demonstration to j██████ists. The F-bike rose off the ground, hovered, █ ██cled around the inside of an exhibition hall for five minutes, carrying a life-size dummy rider. It was flown by remote control.

When can a real person ride the F-bike? Eventually, the inventors hope. Human beings are a lot heavier than the dummy rider, so their flights will require more powerful batteries—and testing time!

ORVILLE AND WILBUR WRIGHT, WHO FLEW THE **FIRST AIRPLANE,** FIRST OWNED A **BIKE REPAIR SHOP.**

TAKES FLIGHT

EACH **YEAR** ABOUT
100
MILLION
NEW BIKES
ARE MADE.

PREFLIGHT PHOTO SESSION

WHAT IN THE
WORLD
HAPPENED HERE?

Each of these four pictures shows a wacky event that happened somewhere in the world. There are three captions with each picture—two fake and one real. Can you pick the real one? You can find the answers on the bottom of page 27. (No peeking!)

1.

1. JILIN, CHINA

A. CITIZEN BRINGS GLACIER HOME FROM A TRIP TO ANTARCTICA.

B. FREAK ICE STORM HITS ONLY ONE SIDE OF A BUILDING.

C. MAN LEAVES THE WATER RUNNING ALL WINTER TO PREVENT FROZEN PIPES; AS A RESULT, WATER FLOWING OUT THE WINDOW CREATES AN ICE TOWER.

2.

2. KOŁOBRZEG, POLAND

A. A TRUCK FULL OF SARDINES OPENS UP AND SPILLS ITS CARGO ALL OVER THE ROAD.

B. FISH FLOP OUT OF A LAKE NEXT TO A ROADWAY.

C. IT'S RAINING TINY FISH.

A RESTAURANT IN WROCŁAW, POLAND, CLAIMS TO HAVE BEEN IN **BUSINESS** FOR MORE THAN **725** YEARS.

3.

FRENCH FRIES *DIPPED* IN **MAYONNAISE** *ARE A* POPULAR **DUTCH** SNACK.

3. AMSTERDAM, NETHERLANDS

A. CONTESTANTS COMPETE FOR "MOST ORANGE" PRIZE IN A HUGE HALLOWEEN CONTEST.

B. SPORTS FANS TRY OUT TO BE THE NATIONAL SOCCER TEAM MASCOT.

C. CITIZENS GATHER OUTSIDE A PALACE TO WELCOME THE COUNTRY'S NEW KING, DRESSED IN THEIR NATIONAL COLOR.

4.

4. BUCHAREST, ROMANIA

A. MEN TAKE THE WORLD'S LARGEST COLLECTION OF DIRTY LAUNDRY TO THE LAUNDROMAT.

B. TWO HUNDRED PEOPLE UNFURL A FLAG THREE TIMES THE SIZE OF A FOOTBALL FIELD, SETTING A GUINNESS WORLD RECORD.

C. CITIZENS BRING OUT THEIR BEST BEDSHEETS FOR A GIANT COLORFUL TUG-OF-WAR CONTEST.

BUCHAREST'S **PALACE OF PARLIAMENT** *IS THE* **LARGEST** (AND **HEAVIEST**) ADMINISTRATIVE BUILDING IN THE WORLD.

ANSWERS: 1.C; 2.A; 3.C; 4.B

CHAPTER 2

WILD
ANIMALS

HTY ANTS SHOW OFF SUPER-DUPER
O WHITE HOUSE • GRUMPY CAT LANDS MOVIE
WKLY (ALMOST) GOES SHOPPING • BEES MOVE
GTON • POLAR BEARS PARTY IN SAN
TWO-LEGGED

CANINE COSTUME CONTEST, PAGE 46

ANIMAL
(MIS) ADVENTURES

FEATHERED HOOLIGAN EJECTED

HERTFORDSHIRE, ENGLAND

What happens when a parrot imitates the referee's whistle at a soccer match? Total chaos! The parrot, named Me-tu, was brought to the game in a cage by his owner. Me-tu started imitating the ref's whistle so convincingly that players would stop playing when they heard it. At first, a referee suspected *a person* was up to mischief. When he discovered Me-tu was the troublemaker, he had to ask the parrot and his owner to leave.

THE WORLD'S OLDEST **PARROT,** AN AFRICAN GRAY, LIVED TO BE **55 YEARS OLD!**

NEWS FEED

>>> **WHITEFIELD, ENGLAND:** A WOMAN TROTTED ON HORSEBACK TO A MCDONALD'S DRIVE-THROUGH WINDOW AND WAS DENIED SERVICE. SO, SHE BROUGHT

STYLISH MONKEY (ALMOST) GOES SHOPPING

TORONTO, CANADA

A tiny monkey dressed in a fashionable coat was found wandering around an IKEA furniture store parking lot. Worried for the frightened monkey's safety, customers ushered him to the store entrance to wait for help. When his owner was found, she told authorities that her monkey, named Darwin, had escaped from his crate in her car. Darwin soon became Canada's most famous shopper!

MONKEYS' TAILS HAVE RIDGES ON THE UNDERSIDE THAT LET THEM PICK UP SOMETHING AS SMALL AS A PEANUT!

A MOOSE'S HUGE ANTLERS ARE DESIGNED TO CHANNEL SOUND TO ITS EARS!

MOOSE SWIMS IN BACKYARD POOL

MANCHESTER, NEW HAMPSHIRE, U.S.A.

One Friday evening, a homeowner in New Hampshire discovered a very unlikely swimmer in his backyard pool: a moose! He called the fire department, and it took a team of nine rescue workers (and plenty of rope) to pull the 1,800-pound (816.5-kg) animal out of the water. As one of the rescuers told the local news station: "I didn't get trained on how to do this, that's for sure. There's a first for everything."

HER HORSE TO THE COUNTER INSIDE THE FAST-FOOD STORE INSTEAD. POLICE WERE SUMMONED IMMEDIATELY AFTER THE HORSE POOPED ON THE RESTAURANT FLOOR.

TWO-LEGGED
"PANDAS"
SPOTTED IN CHINA

PANDAS
POOP
UP TO
50 TIMES
A DAY!

A GIANT **PANDA** IS THE SIZE OF **A STICK OF BUTTER** WHEN IT IS **BORN.**

BRINGING UP BABY

SICHUAN PROVINCE, CHINA

Tao Tao, a baby panda, was born in a Chinese zoo, where he was lovingly raised by his mother, Cao Cao, and some other pandas. These other pandas weighed him and even walked around on two legs. Who were these mysterious pandas? They were costumed scientists, trying to prepare Tao Tao and his mother for life in the wild by limiting their exposure to humans.

Giant pandas are an endangered species; there are only a few thousand left in the world. That's why scientists at China's Wolong National Nature Reserve have been working hard to help zoo pandas like Tao Tao and Cao Cao learn to live independently in their natural habitat.

Before being released into the wild, the two bears were loaded into crates and carried by panda-suited scientists to a remote location in the nature reserve. They were coaxed out of their crates with bamboo shoots and then left to get acquainted with their new surroundings.

As part of the pandas' training, the scientists will show them lifelike models of snow leopards, their natural predators. The models make real leopard growls and roars so Tao Tao and Cao Cao will learn to be afraid of them.

Once their training is complete, the bears will be released into the wild, where, hopefully, they will find other pandas and live long and healthy lives—with little memory of the humans who helped them.

MOTHER'S HELPER

HUMANS IN DISGUISE

JUMBO
THE ELEPHANT TESTS NEW BRIDGE

HEROIC PIGEON DELIVERS MESSAGE

1884

The famous circus elephant Jumbo gave New Yorkers quite a show when he led a herd of 20 elephants (and some camels, too!) across the Brooklyn Bridge. The event was designed to draw audiences to the circus, but it also gave the city a boost of confidence about the strength of its new bridge, which had just opened the year before.

1918

During World War I, the U.S. military used pigeons to deliver messages in dangerous territory. One carrier pigeon named Cher Ami (which means "dear friend" in French) was carrying an important message when he was struck by enemy fire. Despite his injury, Cher Ami kept flying and delivered his message safely, leading to the rescue of 194 trapped soldiers!

>>> ANIMALS, ANIMALS EVERYWHERE

1901

PIG, BEAR, HYENA (AND MORE!) MOVE INTO WHITE HOUSE

When Theodore Roosevelt moved into the White House as president, he brought with him his six children and the largest collection of pets the White House had ever hosted. The Roosevelt children's pets included Maude the pig; a small bear named Jonathan Edwards; as well as a hyena, blue macaw, badger, pony, owl, rabbit, and one-legged rooster!

HAM THE CHIMP CONQUERS SPACE

Before people traveled to space, scientists wondered if humans could survive the trip and think clearly enough to perform tasks in microgravity. A chimp named Ham gave them their answer. Ham was trained to pull levers in response to flashing blue lights. Then he boarded a capsule and rode a rocket into space, where he performed the very same tasks, before safely returning to Earth 16 minutes later. Mission accomplished!

1961

1925

TOGO THE SLED DOG SAVES A RESCUE MISSION

TOGO!

When an epidemic of diphtheria broke out in the remote town of Nome, Alaska, there was only one way to get medicine there—by sending teams of sled dogs across treacherous frozen terrain. A sled dog named Togo was the team leader on the longest and hardest leg of the journey, braving fierce storms and unstable ice. Thanks to Togo's courage and skill, the team made it to Nome and delivered the medicine.

PONY PALACE A BRITISH FAMILY KEEPS THREE MINIATURE HORSES AS HOUSE PETS. THE MINI HORSES ENJOY WATCHING TV AND DRINKING WATER FROM THE KITCHEN TAP. GOOD THING THEY'RE HOUSE-TRAINED!

WACKY
ANIMALS CAUGHT ON CAMERA!

PRETTY IN PINK AUSTRALIA'S NEWLY DISCOVERED SLUGS COME IN A SURPRISING COLOR—HOT PINK! THEY CAN GROW UP TO EIGHT INCHES (20 CM) LONG!

SKUNK SNACK WHEN THIS BABY SKUNK GOT HIS HEAD STUCK IN A YOGURT CONTAINER, A CONNECTICUT HOMEOWNER CALLED AN ANIMAL RESCUE ORGANIZATION, WHICH TUGGED AND TWISTED HIM FREE.

A STRIPED SKUNK'S MUSK CAN BE SMELLED UP TO 1.5 MILES AWAY.
(2.4 km)

ANGRY BIRD AN AGGRESSIVE SWAN SWOOPED DOWN ON A ROWER AND DISRUPTED THE WORLD ROWING CHAMPIONSHIPS IN LAKE BLED, SLOVENIA.

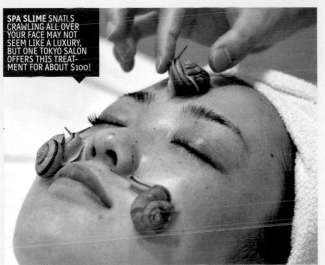

SPA SLIME SNAILS CRAWLING ALL OVER YOUR FACE MAY NOT SEEM LIKE A LUXURY, BUT ONE TOKYO SALON OFFERS THIS TREATMENT FOR ABOUT $100!

A **SNAIL** HAS ABOUT **25,000** TINY **TEETH.**

FREE LUNCH POLICE WERE CALLED TO AN ALASKA GROCERY PARKING LOT WHEN DOZENS OF BALD EAGLES SWARMED A FISH-FILLED PICKUP TRUCK.

FISH IN TRUCK!

POLAR BEARS

SAN FRANCISCO, CALIFORNIA, U.S.A.

San Francisco is famous for its fog, but snow? That's a once (or twice) in a lifetime event in the California city. That's why it was a big surprise when zookeepers at the San Francisco Zoo treated two polar bears to ten tons (more than 9 mT) of snow for their birthdays!

The bears, named Piké and Uulu, awoke one morning in November to find their enclosure filled with artificial snow, which was blown in by a snowmaking machine. The bears rolled, dug, and hung out in the fresh snow. The cold fest got even better when players from the San Francisco Bulls ice hockey team tossed icy fish pucks into the bears' enclosure as birthday snacks.

Piké and Uulu had plenty of reason to celebrate. The usual life span of a polar bear is 15 to 18 years, but Piké and Uulu were celebrating their 30th and 32nd birthdays! That makes them really elderly in the world of polar bears. But as the photos prove, you're never too old to play in the snow!

POLAR PLAYTIME!

UNDER THEIR **FUR,** POLAR BEARS HAVE BLACK **SKIN.**

POLAR BEARS HAVE AN EXTRA, **CLEAR EYELID** THAT HELPS THEM SEE **UNDERWATER,** AND PROTECTS THEIR EYES IN A **SNOWSTORM.**

PARTY IN SNOW
SAN FRANCISCO

A BEAR-Y GOOD TIME!

THE BIRTHDAY BASH WASN'T THE FIRST TIME PIKÉ AND UULU GOT A SNOWY SURPRISE. ONE YEAR, THE ZOOKEEPERS BROUGHT IN SNOW TO CELEBRATE THE ARRIVAL OF WINTER, AND THE BEARS EVEN GOT TO OPEN THEIR OWN CHRISTMAS PRESENT!

GRUMPY CAT LANDS MOVIE DEAL

FAMOUS FACE

MORRISTOWN, ARIZONA, U.S.A.

Grumpy Cat, the feline Web celeb, has scored her first major movie deal. The crabby-faced kitty, whose real name is Tardar Sauce, will speak in the movie (thanks to special effects). The frowny feline has also appeared on TV and was featured in a book called *Grumpy Cat*. Has all this fame given her reason to smile? Not at all. Talk about a sourpuss!

LADYBUG MALL MADNESS

WHO 72,000 LADYBUGS

WHAT THE INSECTS WERE RELEASED INSIDE THE MALL OF AMERICA, ONE OF THE LARGEST MALLS IN THE U.S.A.

WHERE BLOOMINGTON, MINNESOTA, U.S.A.

HOW SCHOOLCHILDREN GENTLY HELPED SPOON OUT THE LADYBUGS ONTO THE LEAVES OF THE MALL'S INDOOR PLANTS.

WHY LADYBUGS EAT APHIDS, WHICH WERE INFESTING THE PLANTS. LADYBUGS ARE BETTER THAN BUG SPRAY BECAUSE THEY'RE FRIENDLIER TO PLANTS AND PEOPLE!

NEWS FEED

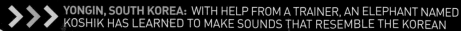

>>> **YONGIN, SOUTH KOREA:** WITH HELP FROM A TRAINER, AN ELEPHANT NAMED KOSHIK HAS LEARNED TO MAKE SOUNDS THAT RESEMBLE THE KOREAN

OCTOPUS CAUSES BLACKOUT

COBURG, GERMANY

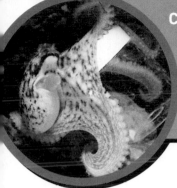

Overnight surveillance at an aquarium in Germany revealed that Otto the octopus was to blame for several mysterious power outages. No one knew what was causing havoc with the building's electrical system until the video footage was studied. Otto was caught in the act of climbing onto the rim of his tank and spraying a stream of water at an offensively bright light. No doubt just trying to get some shut-eye!

BEES MOVE INTO SHINY NEW "SKYSCRAPER"

BEE-UTIFUL NEW HOME!

BUFFALO, NEW YORK, U.S.A.

Honeybees have a cool new home, thanks to winners of a design contest. Their stainless steel tower stands 22 feet (6.7 m) high. The bees live in glass-and-wooden boxes partway up the tower. Beekeepers can lower the boxes to see how the bees are doing. And when you step into the tower—which has perforated walls that bees can enter and exit from—you can look up and imagine what it would be like to be a bee in a beehive!

WORDS FOR "HELLO," "GOOD," "NO," AND "SIT DOWN." KOSHIK TUCKS HIS TRUNK INTO HIS MOUTH TO "SPEAK."

MIGHTY ANTS SHOW OFF *SUPER-DUPER* STRENGTH

VIETNAM

Weaver ants are known for their lifting ability—they can use their jaws to lift items that are a hundred times their own weight! A Vietnamese photographer decided to test these skills by giving the ants bigger and bigger items to carry. After the ants successfully hauled flowers, leaves, pieces of paper, bits of coconut, and also whole chili peppers, the photographer tried these colored pencils. This weight-lifting feat is the equivalent of a person carrying 19,000 pounds (8,618 kg) with his teeth!

ONE SHEEP, SIX YEARS, *TWENTY SUITS*

SOUTH ISLAND, NEW ZEALAND

Shrek the sheep became quite the celebrity in New Zealand after spending six years hiding out in caves. Some say he went "on the lam" to escape shearing. When finally captured and shorn, not only was he much cooler, his fleece contained enough wool to make 20 business suits.

CAT TRAVELS 200 MILES TO GET HOME

WHO A FOUR-YEAR-OLD INDOOR CAT NAMED HOLLY

WHAT LOST DURING A FAMILY VACATION, HOLLY REMARKABLY REAPPEARED IN HER HOMETOWN, TWO WHOLE MONTHS LATER!

WHERE FLORIDA, U.S.A.

HOW HOLLY APPARENTLY WALKED 200 MILES (322 KM) FROM DAYTONA BEACH TO WEST PALM BEACH, FLORIDA. NO ONE CAN FIGURE OUT HOW SHE DID IT, BUT SOME SPECULATE THE CAT KNEW TO KEEP THE OCEAN TO HER LEFT AS SHE WALKED SOUTH.

WHY THERE'S NO PLACE LIKE HOME.

NEWS FEED

>>> CHICAGO, ILLINOIS, U.S.A.: A CREW OF 25 ANIMALS, INCLUDING GOATS, LLAMAS, AND SHEEP, WERE HIRED TO CHOMP AND CHEW THEIR WAY

SAILOR SPOTS REAL-LIFE "MOBY DICK"

OFF THE NORWAY COAST

While out at sea, a British man grabbed his camera when he spotted an extremely rare creature—a white humpback whale! The usual dark gray pigment of humpback whales was missing everywhere except for a small black splash underneath its tail. The man named the whale Willow and said it was the sight of a lifetime. That's because white whales are not only rare, they're legendary! Moby Dick, the star of Herman Melville's famous novel, was a white sperm whale.

LABRADOODLE MISTAKEN FOR LION

ROAR!

NORFOLK, VIRGINIA, U.S.A.

Confused and frightened citizens dialed police when they spied a rambunctious labradoodle not far from the Virginia Zoo. That's because they thought they were seeing a baby lion on the loose. With his fancy lion look-alike haircut and dyed mane and tail, Charles the Monarch fooled everyone!

THROUGH OVERGROWN GRASS AND WEEDS AT O'HARE AIRPORT. WHY THE ANIMALS? THEY'RE MUCH QUIETER THAN LAWN MOWERS—AND BETTER FOR THE ENVIRONMENT.

CANINE
COSTUME **CONTEST**

What's cuter than a dog in costume? Not much! These masquerading mutts have been gathered from all over the globe. It's up to you to name the winner by conducting your very own Pooch Poll!

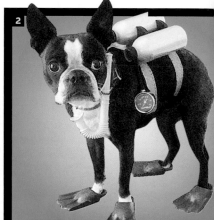

PRICEY **PUP** "WEDDING"

NEW YORK CITY, NEW YORK, U.S.A.

One July evening at a hotel near Central Park, a little dog named Baby Hope Diamond got married to a tie-dyed poodle named Chilly Pasternak. For her special day, Baby Hope donned a $6,000 designer dress! The event was a fund-raiser for the Humane Society of New York. It cost more than $158,000 to put on, setting the world record for the most expensive pet wedding ever. Holy *mutt*rimony!

HOW TO CONDUCT A POOCH POLL

POLLS ARE A GOOD WAY TO TAKE A READING OF PEOPLES' OPINIONS. BUT TO GET A GOOD READING, POLLSTERS HAVE TO USE SPECIAL TECHNIQUES. HERE'S HOW YOU CAN CONDUCT A PERFECT POOCH POLL.

1. WRITE THE NUMBERS 1-8 ON A SHEET OF PAPER.

2. SHOW THE CANINE COSTUME CONTEST PHOTOS TO A FRIEND OR FAMILY MEMBER. ASK HIM OR HER TO PICK THEIR FAVORITE. MARK THE CHOICE ON YOUR PAPER.

3. ASK MORE FRIENDS OR FAMILY MEMBERS FOR THEIR VOTES. TAKE CARE TO ASK EACH PERSON PRIVATELY, AND DON'T LET ANYONE SEE THE OTHER VOTES. PEER PRESSURE CAN INFLUENCE THE RESULTS!

4. AFTER YOU'VE TALKED TO AT LEAST TEN PEOPLE, ADD UP YOUR VOTES. WHICH POOCH PREVAILS?

CHAPTER 3

INCREDIBLE
INVENTIONS

BOT CAMERA FACES DANGEROUS ANIMALS · CRE
OBOTS DETECT BODY ODOR · COMMERCIALS
ERGY PROBLEMS · NORWEGIAN TOWN BRIGHTEN
TELL ME A STORY · PAJAMAS · SOCK
SED WATER · FLASH

SPIDER BOTS, PAGE 58

INTO THE WILD

SAY CHEESE!

ROBOT CAMERA FACES DANGEROUS ANIMALS

KENYA

What happens when rolling robots in camouflage approach animals in the wild? They take great wildlife photos! Developed by English brothers Matt and Will Burrard-Lucas, the BeetleCam is a remote-controlled camera that gets close-up shots of wild animals. The brothers tested their camera in Kenya's Masai Mara National Reserve, where lions were so curious about the gadget that they walked right up to it. The BeetleCam even survived being mauled and carried off into the bush by the big cats.

NASA'S CURIOSITY ROVER TAKES PICTURES ON MARS USING 17 DIFFERENT CAMERAS.

NEWS FEED

>>> MIAMI, FLORIDA, U.S.A.: iPADS ARE NOT JUST FOR HUMANS ANYMORE! AT MIAMI'S JUNGLE ISLAND ZOO, ORANGUTANS ARE GIVEN iPADS TO HELP

CREEPY CRAWLER

HAMPSHIRE, ENGLAND >>>

Animatronics expert Matt Denton has designed and created the ultimate "entertainment vehicle"— a giant robot bug. It took four years and a lot of money for Denton to develop this science fiction–inspired toy, but by early 2013 it was road ready. Even a marine research organization and a mining company have expressed interest in the unique robot. But don't expect speed from this bug. The lumbering beast can only travel one mile (1.6 km) an hour. Denton doesn't mind at all. "It wasn't built to be efficient and fast," he said. "It was built to look cool and insectlike and fun." Mission accomplished!

MORE THAN **100** SEARCH-AND-RESCUE DOGS *HELPED LOOK FOR* **SURVIVORS** *AFTER THE* **9/11** *ATTACK ON THE WORLD TRADE CENTER IN* **NEW YORK CITY.**

CALLING ALL BIOBOTS

<<< RESCUE ROACHES

NORTH CAROLINA, U.S.A.

Could cockroaches—those insects that everyone loves to hate—one day save people's lives? That's what researchers are hoping, thanks to an invention called "biobot" technology. Scientists at North Carolina State University wired cockroaches with electrodes placed on their antennae, and added a tiny backpack containing wireless controls to their backs with a magnet. They are hoping the roaches will someday carry sound detectors or tiny cameras so they can search out earthquake victims trapped in rubble. Roaches to the rescue!

THEM COMMUNICATE AND LEARN. JUNGLE ISLAND IS JUST ONE OF SEVERAL ZOOS EXPERIMENTING WITH COMPUTERS AND APES.

AVATAR A
2015–2020

In the first step, scientists make a remote-controlled robot that is a copy of the human body.

A FRENCH WOMAN NAMED **JEANNE CALMENT** **LIVED TO BE 122,** MAKING HER THE **OLDEST PERSON** WITH A VERIFIED BIRTH RECORD.

AVATAR B
2020–2025

Next, a human brain is transplanted into the computerized human, or avatar, when the human dies.

HOW TO LIVE FOREVER

STEP ONE: BECOME A ROBOT

MOSCOW, RUSSIA

Believe it or not, humans may one day be able to live forever! At least that's the thinking of a Russian multimillionaire named Dmitry Itskov. He has a technology in the works that he hopes will allow him to become something like a living robot.

AVATAR C
2030–2035

The human brain will be made into an artificial brain with consciousness and personality, and placed into the avatar.

AVATAR D
2040–2045

The avatar and its humanlike brain will be made into a hologram and "live" forever.

TO CREATE HUMAN-LOOKING ROBOT HEADS, DAVID HANSON OF DALLAS, TEXAS, U.S.A., USES A SKINLIKE MATERIAL HE INVENTED CALLED FRUBBER.

THE INSIDE OF THIS ROBOT HEAD WILL BE FITTED WITH MOTORS THAT WILL MAKE THE FACIAL EXPRESSIONS WORK.

Itskov plans to have his brain uploaded to a human-shaped avatar, or computerized figure. That avatar would then one day be turned into a hologram, or "body of light," with all of the smarts and personality of a real person. Itskov hopes the process will be complete by 2045. But a few milestones and inventions must happen along the way, as described in the series of avatars above.

Itskov founded an organization called the 2045 Initiative to help his dream of immortality become reality. While the project is considered far-fetched by many, Itskov hopes the technologies it creates will lead to a new kind of evolution for humans. Ready to sign up?

THE **LONGEST LIVING** ANIMAL, A QUAHOG CLAM, **LIVED** FOR **507** YEARS.

ROBOTS *DETECT* BODY ODOR

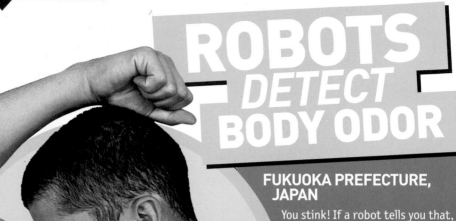

FUKUOKA PREFECTURE, JAPAN

You stink! If a robot tells you that, don't be offended—it's just doing its job. It's an odor-detecting robot developed by scientists at a Japanese university. Kaori-chan is a female robot head who smells your breath and gives answers such as "Like citrus," or "Yuck!" or "I can't stand it!" Place your feet near the foot-sniffing dog Shuntaro-kun, and he'll react to the level of stink in your feet. He might nestle up to you if you smell good. Or, he may bark or fall to the ground if he doesn't like what he smells. If you don't like the responses, don't blame the odor-sniffing robots. They're programmed to be totally honest.

NORWEGIAN TOWN BRIGHTENS UP— WITH GIANT MIRRORS

WHO RESIDENTS OF NORWEGIAN VALLEY TOWN

WHAT INSTALL MIRRORS TO REFLECT LIGHT ON THEIR TOWN

WHERE RJUKAN, NORWAY

WHY BECAUSE OF ITS VALLEY

LOCATION, THE TINY TOWN GETS NO DIRECT SUNLIGHT FROM SEPTEMBER TO MARCH. THE SURROUNDING MOUNTAINS CAST LONG SHADOWS OVER THE TOWN, MAKING FOR VERY GLOOMY WINTERS. TO GET THEMSELVES OUT OF THE DARK, THE TOWN INSTALLED MIRRORS TO REFLECT THE SUN'S LIGHT FROM THE MOUNTAINS INTO THE VALLEY TOWN BELOW. THE ANGLE OF THE MIRRORS IS ADJUSTED THROUGHOUT THE DAY TO DELIVER MAXIMUM SUNLIGHT.

NEWS FEED

>>> **JOHANNESBURG, SOUTH AFRICA:** FACIAL-RECOGNITION TECHNOLOGY IS NOW AT WORK AT A COFFEE-VENDING MACHINE AT JOHANNESBURG'S

COMMERCIALS *SHOT INTO* YOUR SKULL

UNTERFÖHRING, GERMANY

One day, that voice inside your head might not be your own! The German broadcaster Sky Deutschland has tested a system that transmits ads through vibrating train windows. Passengers resting their heads against the window, perhaps to fall asleep, instead heard a voice that urged them to download an app on their smartphone. A device on the window delivered sound to the inner ear by passing vibrations through the skull. This technology sounds cool, but many people consider it an invasion of privacy. Would you want a commercial blasted straight into your head?

ARTIFICIAL LEAF *MAY SOLVE* ENERGY *PROBLEMS*

CAMBRIDGE, MASSACHUSETTS, U.S.A.

What if a leaf were the answer to the world's energy problems? Harvard University professor Daniel Nocera has developed a way to imitate the solar energy process of photosynthesis, Earth's natural energy maker. The artificial leaf is a silicon wafer coated with materials that use sunlight to turn water into hydrogen and oxygen—just like a real leaf does. Just one leaf, along with sunlight and a bottle and a half of drinking water, can create enough energy to power a small home. One day the leaf technology may be able to help the 1.2 billion people worldwide living without electricity.

O. R. TAMBO INTERNATIONAL AIRPORT. WHEN THE MACHINE DETECTS SOMEONE YAWNING IN FRONT OF IT, IT DISPENSES A FREE CUP OF COFFEE.

WEARABLE TECH

SET YOUR "SPIDEY SENSE" TINGLING

CHICAGO, ILLINOIS, U.S.A.

Ever wish you had the super-senses of Spider-Man? Now you can! Researchers at the University of Illinois at Chicago have developed the SpiderSense suit, which has 13 sensors around the body. When something comes near, the sensors place pressure on the wearer's skin. The pressure increases as the object gets closer. The suit has a 95 percent success rate in detecting movement near the wearer, so you'll be ready for that battle in a dark alley. A more practical use, however, is to help those with vision or hearing impairments, or to guide cyclists in traffic. So in some ways, it really does provide super-powers. No radioactive spider necessary!

SPECIALIZED **HAIRS** HELP **SPIDERS** TELL THE DIFFERENCE BETWEEN A *GUST OF WIND* AND AN **APPROACHING PREDATOR.**

NEWS FEED

>>> **SITKA, ALASKA, U.S.A.:** CAN'T REMEMBER DATES? THEN LET THE REMEMBER RING DO IT FOR YOU. AN ALASKA JEWELRY COMPANY IS DEVELOPING A

TELL ME A STORY, PAJAMAS

IDAHO FALLS, IDAHO, U.S.A.

Some kids wear bedtime stories all over themselves—which look like polka dots. Just scan one of the patterns of dots on the child's pj's and get ready for a tale. Each pattern registers a different story, complete with words and pictures, which can be seen on a smartphone or iPad. And a free app reads the stories aloud to you. The pajamas, from a company based in Idaho, are available for boys and girls from ages one to ten. Sleep tight, young techie!

KIDS LEARN AS MANY AS 12,000 NEW WORDS A YEAR JUST FROM READING BOOKS.

YOU CAN BUY SOCKS THAT KEEP TRACK OF HOW YOU RUN AND HOW LONG YOU RUN.

SOCK IT TO ME!

ZÜRICH, SWITZERLAND

>>>

If you haven't quite got your footwear in gear, here's something that might help. The Smarter Socks system, a subscription service of a Swiss company called Blacksocks, delivers crisp, new socks to customers. Each sock has a computer chip in it. When you scan the chip, it lets you—and the company—know how old each sock is, which foot it belongs on, and how many times it's been washed. When the socks wear out, new ones are delivered. And the "blackometer" function alerts you when the socks begin to fade. You'll never have holey socks again!

RING WITH A MICROCHIP IN IT THAT WILL CAUSE THE RING TO HEAT UP EVERY HOUR FOR 24 HOURS BEFORE A BIG EVENT. NOW THAT'S A HOT IDEA!

SPiDER
BOTS

COMING SOON TO A BODY NEAR YOU

NEW YORK CITY, NEW YORK, U.S.A.

AN ARMY OF MICROSCOPIC ROBOTS IS STANDING BY, ready to help the human body. Thanks to nanotechnology, a branch of science that deals with the terrifically tiny, these bots are 100,000 times smaller than the diameter of a human hair. Why would people want armies of robots in their bodies? Simply put, to police the body and zap the bad guys. These robots will walk like spiders along cell surfaces and be programmed to spot problems and fix them. They can be programmed to walk straight, or turn left or right. Once inside the body, the bots could be ordered to clean arteries, fix damaged tissue, and even blast away cancer cells. That's a megajob for such a microscopic creation!

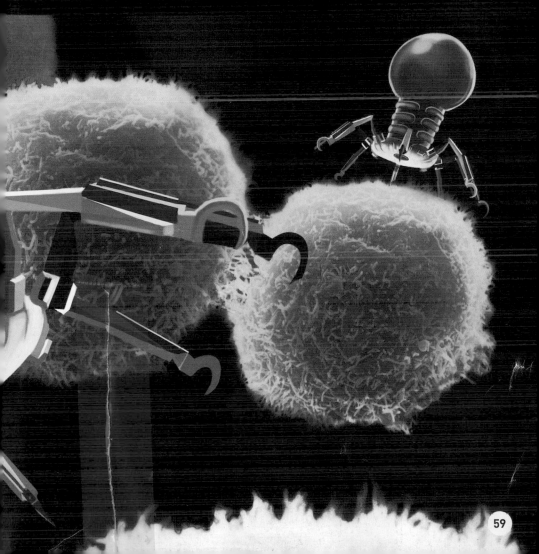

AIR-QUALITY BALLOONS HOW'S THE AIR YOU'RE BREATHING? A SENSOR HOOKED TO A TRICOLORED LED INSIDE THESE BALLOONS LETS YOU KNOW. LIKE A TRAFFIC LIGHT, THE GREEN, YELLOW, AND RED LIGHTS INDICATE GOOD, FAIR, AND POOR AIR QUALITY.

[Bright Ideas]

LED (or light-emitting diode) lights have been around for a while, but never like this. Here are some innovative ways that LED technologies are pioneering the stranger side of lighting.

LED LIGHTS
USE AT LEAST
75 PERCENT
LESS **ENERGY**
THAN REGULAR,
INCANDESCENT
BULBS.

COLOR-CODED WATER DON'T GET BURNED OR ICED! RED-COLORED HOT WATER AND BLUE-COLORED COLD WATER HELP KEEP FOLKS SAFE—AND CLEAN! IT WON'T STAIN YOUR HANDS BECAUSE IT'S JUST A LIGHT!

LIGHT UP LASHES
THESE FUNKY EYELASHES
CAN LIGHT UP YOUR
WORLD. HOW DO YOU
TURN THEM ON OR OFF?
JUST TILT YOUR HEAD!

FLASH DANCE A BRIDE LIGHTS UP
THE DANCE FLOOR IN A WEDDING
DRESS STUDDED WITH LEDS.

COOL RIDE THESE LIGHTS
ARE FOR KEEPING RIDERS
SAFE AND FOR GRABBING
ATTENTION. THE MONKEY
LIGHT BIKE LIGHT SYSTEM
TRANSFORMS BIKE WHEELS
INTO AMAZING COLOR
DISPLAYS OF MOVING IMAGES.

THE **DIODES**
IN LED LIGHTS
ARE ABOUT THE
SIZE OF A
FLECK OF
PEPPER.

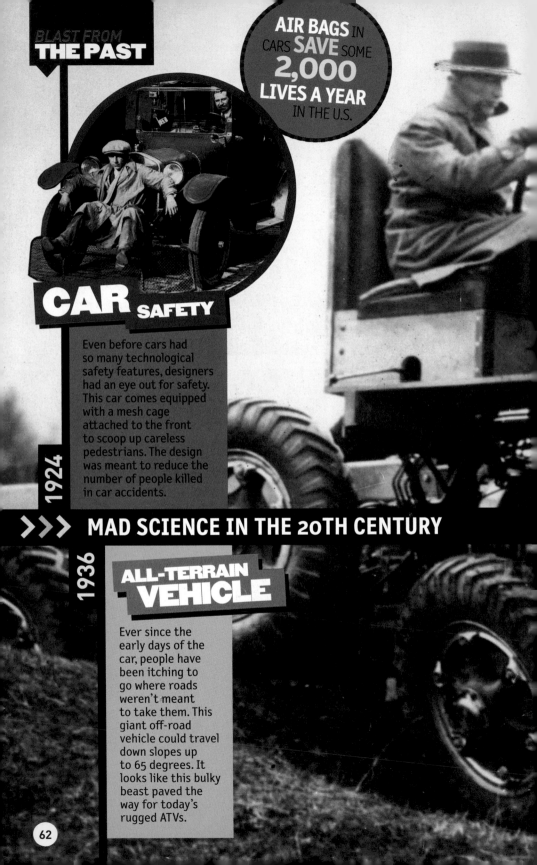

AIR BAGS IN CARS **SAVE** SOME **2,000** LIVES A YEAR IN THE U.S.

CAR SAFETY

1924

Even before cars had so many technological safety features, designers had an eye out for safety. This car comes equipped with a mesh cage attached to the front to scoop up careless pedestrians. The design was meant to reduce the number of people killed in car accidents.

>>> MAD SCIENCE IN THE 20TH CENTURY

1936

ALL-TERRAIN VEHICLE

Ever since the early days of the car, people have been itching to go where roads weren't meant to take them. This giant off-road vehicle could travel down slopes up to 65 degrees. It looks like this bulky beast paved the way for today's rugged ATVs.

A SUPERLIGHT **GPS DEVICE** CAN BE USED TO **TRACK** WHERE YOUR **PET CAT** TRAVELS DURING THE DAY.

RADIO HAT

1931

This guy would have loved the iPod! It wasn't long after the invention of radio broadcasts that people tried to take their clunky radios with them. This portable radio is built into a straw hat, picking up radio signals right above your head. It comes complete with a horn to deliver the sounds to you.

EARLY GPS

1932

Today, global positioning systems, or GPS's, help drivers know where to go without having to get out a paper map. This early version of a GPS uses a much lower tech method—a rolling map. The system connects to a car's dashboard and a screen shows a map that rolls at the same rate that your car moves.

FAXED NEWSPAPER

1938

Extra! Extra! Electronic newspapers are old news! These kids are poring over a paper delivered without help from the paperboy. Instead, it was sent via radio signals to a special device that printed out the pages, much like today's fax machines. But the early device was so slow and noisy, it didn't catch on. Traditional paper delivery remained the rule until the rise of the Internet.

63

WRINKLE YOUR NOSE, STICK OUT YOUR TONGUE

TO UNLOCK YOUR SMART-PHONE ...

MOUNTAIN VIEW, CALIFORNIA, U.S.A.

Smartphones may soon ask users to play Simon Says. Facial recognition software already allows Google Face Unlock to unlock smartphones just by flashing your face in front of it. But hackers can bypass the system by putting a photo in front of the phone instead of the real thing. So Google has patented a new technology that will require the user to make predetermined movements in front of the screen to unlock it. Blink, wink, raise an eyebrow, or stick out your tongue, smartphone owners. Show your phone who you are!

SCIENTISTS CREATE SUPERWORM ROBOT

WHO RESEARCHERS AT HARVARD UNIVERSITY, MASSACHUSETTS INSTITUTE OF TECHNOLOGY, AND SEOUL NATIONAL UNIVERSITY

WHAT MESHWORM, AN EARTHWORM ROBOT

WHERE CAMBRIDGE, MASSACHUSETTS, U.S.A., AND SEOUL, SOUTH KOREA

WHY SCIENTISTS WANTED TO MAKE A ROBOT OF SOFT MATERIALS THAT ARE NEARLY INDE-STRUCTIBLE. THE ROBOT MESHWORM MOVES BY CONTRACTING SEGMENTS OF ITS BODY, SIMILAR TO A WORM. A BOT LIKE MESHWORM COULD BE USED TO NAVIGATE ROUGH SURFACES AND MOVE THROUGH TIGHT SPACES.

NEWS FEED

>>> **WEST LAFAYETTE, INDIANA, U.S.A.:** SCIENTISTS AT PURDUE UNIVERSITY ARE WORKING ON A "TIME CLOAK"—A DEVICE THAT BENDS LIGHT TO

COULD *FUTURE* HUMANS *BE* BUG-EYED *AND* BIG BRAINED?

PITTSBURGH, PENNSYLVANIA, U.S.A.

What might humans look like in, say, 100,000 years? An artist and scientist have teamed up to explore just that. The human brain will continue to develop and grow, making our foreheads larger, speculates scientist Alan Kwan. But he predicts that our earthly environment will change, too. And if living on other planets is in our distant future, larger eyes will be needed to adapt to being farther from the sun—and eyelids to the sides of our eyes instead of on top will help protect our eyes from the cosmic rays in space. Will the future make us superhuman, or super strange-looking? Pittsburgh artist Nickolay Lamm has drawn it, so you decide.

ROCHESTER, NEW YORK, U.S.A.

When Harry Potter slips into an invisibility cloak, it seems like pure magic. But some scientists feel they are close to making such a cloak a reality—and space satellites may be the first objects to hide behind them. One idea, called transformation optics, uses new materials to guide light around objects, as if they weren't there. Another idea involves bending light around a region of space with simple lenses and mirrors. While the tech isn't quite ready yet, scientists are hopeful that with a little more work, they can soon make stuff disappear!

SPACE SATELLITE

SATELLITES *IN SPACE* *MAY TAKE A* LESSON *FROM* HARRY POTTER

TEAR A TINY HOLE IN TIME, ENABLING THEM TO HIDE UNDETECTABLE SECRET MESSAGES A FRACTION OF A SECOND LONG.

SPACE INVADERS

Did you know that some common objects on Earth are made of materials that were first invented for space travel? Match each of these space technologies with the everyday item below that uses that same space tech. You can find the answers on the bottom of page 67.

IN 2008 AN **ASTRONAUT** **LOST A TOOL BAG** WORTH *$100,000* ON A **SPACE WALK.**

1. Heat-seeking missile trackers have a nearly clear protector for their antennas that's made of a material called translucent polycrystalline alumina, or TPA. How do we use this translucent material on Earth?

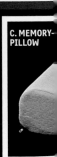

2. When dirt and particles in space began scratching astronauts' helmet visors, inventors came up with a scratch-resistant coating. What common item do we coat with this material here on Earth to prevent scratches?

A. CELL PHONE

B. SMOKE DETECTOR

C. MEMORY-PILLOW

SATELLITES ARE USED TO MEASURE THE **TEMPERATURE** OF THE **OCEANS** AND TRACK **CLIMATE CHANGE.**

3. These supercomfy seats are also a safety feature. A material called open-cell polymeric foam was invented to help give astronauts a safer landing. How is this cozy spring-back material used at home today?

4. Satellites are *the* way to communicate over super-duper long distances. NASA uses them to transmit info about outer space back to Earth. Now more than 200 communication satellites orbit Earth each day. What are they used for?

THREE CREWS OF **ASTRONAUTS** SPENT **171 DAYS** **ORBITING** EARTH IN **SKYLAB.**

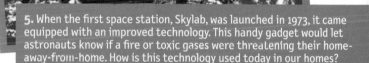

5. When the first space station, Skylab, was launched in 1973, it came equipped with an improved technology. This handy gadget would let astronauts know if a fire or toxic gases were threatening their home-away-from-home. How is this technology used today in our homes?

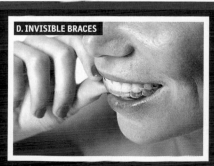

D. INVISIBLE BRACES

E. SCRATCH-RESISTANT LENSES

CHAPTER 4

FREAKY
FOOD

"ON TOP OF SPAGHETTI" BECOMES
L-O IS BORN • EXPLORER EATS 36,000-YEAR-OLD ICE A
STO • VIENNESE ORCHESTRA CARVES THEIR O
IDENT • MOST EXPENSIVE COFFEE IS MADE FROM EL
WITH YOUR FOOD •

CANDY-EATING
COWS, PAGE 74

GEORGE WASHINGTON–SHAPED CHICKEN NUGGET GOES FOR BIG BUCKS

MUST-SEE PHOTO!

SIOUX CITY, IOWA, U.S.A.

How much would you pay for a three-year-old frozen chicken nugget that looks like the first president of the United States? The nugget in question was put up for auction on eBay as a fund-raiser for a children's summer camp, and the presidential poultry product earned 71 bids before selling for $8,100. Unfortunately, however, the deal fell through. The winning bidder chickened out.

FRENCH-FRIED TAXI

WHO AN ECO-FRIENDLY TAXI COMPANY CALLED RECAB

WHAT TURNED OLD CARS INTO TAXIS TO RUN ON FUEL MADE FROM USED FRENCH-FRY OIL

WHERE BOISE, IDAHO, U.S.A.

HOW THE USED FRENCH-FRY OIL IS COLLECTED FROM LOCAL RESTAURANTS AND PURIFIED INTO BIODIESEL TO RUN THE OLD MERCEDES-BENZ SEDANS.

WHY BIODIESEL PRODUCES LESS CARBON DIOXIDE EMISSION THAN REGULAR DIESEL FUEL, AND THE USED FRENCH-FRY OIL WOULD OTHERWISE HAVE BEEN WASTED. BONUS: BIODIESEL IS MUCH CHEAPER THAN REGULAR FUEL.

NEWS FEED

>>> CENTRAL TEXAS: WHILE DOCTORS MAY DISAGREE, TEXAS RESIDENT PEARL CANTRELL SAYS THAT EATING BACON EVERY DAY IS THE REASON

HAMBURGER *FLIES INTO* SPACE

STURBRIDGE, MASSACHUSETTS, U.S.A.

Five Harvard University students made history when they hitched a hamburger to a weather balloon and launched it into space. Equipped with a camera and a GPS device, the burger took a two-hour flight, reaching an altitude of 19 miles (30.6 km) before plummeting back to Earth. The burger landed in a tree 130 miles (209 km) from the launch site. It took a few days (and a hired tree climber) to get the burger down, and then the students got their reward—amazing video footage of the world's first astroburger!

ASTRO-BURGER

SPAIN HOSTS GINORMOUS GRAPE FIGHT

MALLORCA, SPAIN

Every September, crowds flock to the quiet village of Binissalem on the isle of Mallorca for a grape-throwing food fight. More than a thousand people form a circle around a massive heap of grapes, and when the whistle blows, grapes start flying, clothes turn purple, and the ground gets soaked with juice. The tradition began as a way to celebrate the harvest and, some say, to get rid of grapes that weren't good enough to be made into wine.

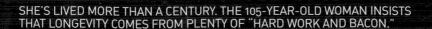

SHE'S LIVED MORE THAN A CENTURY. THE 105-YEAR-OLD WOMAN INSISTS THAT LONGEVITY COMES FROM PLENTY OF "HARD WORK AND BACON."

ITALIAN CHEFS MAKE WORLD'S

ROME, ITALY

FIVE CHEFS IN ITALY JOINED FORCES to smash a pizza pie record set in South Africa. Measuring 131 feet (40 m) across, the pizza took 48 hours to bake and was assembled from 5,000 batches of dough. Ingredients included 9.9 tons (8.9 mT) of flour, 5 tons (4.5 mT) of tomato sauce, 8,800 pounds (4 mT) of mozzarella, and 275 pounds (125 kg) of parmesan. Now that's a big pie!

LARGEST ROUND PIZZA

SWEET
SENSATIONS

THAT'S WEIRD!

CANDY-EATING COWS

U.S.A.

Cows usually dine on grass, corn, and other grains, but as the cost of corn rises, some farmers are swapping out corn for candy! Cows are now munching on chocolate bars, gummy worms, cookie crumbs, marshmallows, and hot chocolate mix. Farmers say the treats are a good replacement for the sugar naturally found in corn, and that the cows—and their milk and meat—are not harmed by their sweets-infused diet.

IT TAKES **400 CACAO BEANS** TO MAKE **1 POUND** (453.6 g) OF **CHOCOLATE.**

NEWS FEED

>>> **BAKERSFIELD, CALIFORNIA, U.S.A.:** A TEAM OF CALIFORNIA FRUIT BREEDERS HAS INVENTED COTTON CANDY–FLAVORED GRAPES! THEY LOOK JUST

TIRED OF GUMMY BEARS? MAKE A GUMMY YOU!

TOKYO, JAPAN

FabCafe in Tokyo offers customers a unique treat: gummy candy in their own image! To create your gummy self, you stand in front of a 3-D body scanner. Then a 3-D printer produces an action-figure-size silicone model of you. This model is used to make a candy mold. When the mold is ready, you pour a liquid gummy mixture into it. In just a few hours, the gel has set, and a little gummy person in your image is born!

GUMMY BEARS WERE ORIGINALLY CALLED "DANCING BEARS."

45,000 TONS OF (40,823 mT) MARSHMALLOWS ARE SOLD IN THE U.S. EVERY YEAR.
THAT'S AS MUCH AS 225 BLUE WHALES!

CHOCOLATIER MAKES LIFE-SIZE CHOCOLATE SHOES

DALLAS, TEXAS, U.S.A.

Master chocolatier Andrea Pedraza loves designer high heels as much as she loves chocolate. So she put her two passions together and created a delicious collection of life-size chocolate shoes! The decadent pumps, which sell for $30 to $55 each, are especially popular as Valentine's Day gifts.

LIKE REGULAR GREEN GRAPES, BUT WHEN YOU POP ONE IN YOUR MOUTH, IT TASTES LIKE THAT AIRY CONFECTION FAMILIAR TO ALL AMUSEMENT PARK AND CIRCUS FANS.

BICYCLE ▶

CHEERYO

[PLAY WITH YOUR FOOD]

For 50 years, New Yorker Bill Wurtzel entertained his wife by whipping up hilarious—and healthy—breakfasts for her. Here are some of his master-pieces. Try playing with your food to see what creations *you* can make!

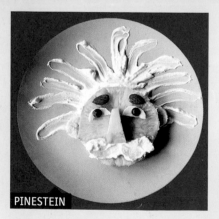

PINESTEIN

ASTRONAUTS
ON THE APOLLO 11
MISSION TO THE MOON
ATE BACON
SQUARES
AND **PEACHES** FOR BREAKFAST.

INFLATED EGGO

PIT DRUMMER

CEREAL IS THE MOST COMMON **BREAKFAST** **FOOD** IN THE **U.S.** IN JAPAN, IT'S *SOUP!*

CHEW CHEW

BEANHEAD

PUMPKIN

CRACK OPEN THE PUMPKIN TOP.

CARVE OUT THE INSIDES.

CLIMB ABOARD AND START ROWING!

CANADA AND U.S.A.

What can you do with a pumpkin that weighs more than 1,500 pounds (680 kg)? You could try to win a giant pumpkin contest. Or you could make a whole lot of pumpkin pie. But here's another idea—you could race it in a pumpkin regatta!

Pumpkin racing has been gathering fans across the United States and Canada. Overgrown pumpkins that are big enough to sit in are carved and hollowed out just like jack-o'-lanterns. Sometimes chain saws are required to help with the job.

Competitors show up on race day, and when the countdown begins, they take off, paddling like mad. Forget staying in any lanes. The goal is to stay afloat and steer that pumpkin boat around a buoy and back to the starting line.

Spectators along the shore cheer on the paddlers as they try to steer their unwieldy crafts. After all, they're not exactly sleek racing vessels. In the end all the participants are champions, and the once awesome pumpkins are usually hauled off to the compost heap.

EXPLORER EATS 36,000-YEAR-OLD ICE AGE BISON MEAT

1979

Alaska paleontologist Dale Guthrie and his team found a 36,000-year-old bison frozen in the icy ground near Fairbanks, Alaska, U.S.A. They were amazed to find that it was very well preserved—so well preserved that there was flesh on its bones! Guthrie and his team celebrated their discovery by cooking a small bit of flesh from the bison's neck in a stew. How did it taste? Very chewy!

1979

1983 PRESIDENT SENDS JELLY BEANS ON SPACE MISSION

U.S. president Ronald Reagan was such a fan of jelly beans, he always kept a jar in the Oval Office and another one on *Air Force One*. When Reagan wanted to send the astronauts of the space shuttle *Challenger* a special surprise, he chose his signature collection of red, white, and blue jelly beans. Besides the beans, *Challenger* also carried Sally Ride, America's first female astronaut.

YOU CAN BUY **JELLY BEANS** IN THESE FLAVORS: **PENCIL SHAVINGS**, **SKUNK SPRAY**, **MOLDY CHEESE**, AND **BOOGER**.

CHEF DISHES

DIRT-DRESSED SALAD

A SPOONFUL OF **DIRT** CONTAINS MORE **ORGANISMS** THAN THERE ARE PEOPLE ON **EARTH.**

DIRT ICE CREAM

DIRT

MUD ON THE MENU!

DIRT SOUP

FORKS
WEREN'T COMMONLY USED FOR **EATING** UNTIL THE 19TH CENTURY.

TOYKO, JAPAN

Imagine walking into a nice French restaurant. You sit down at the beautifully set table, and the waiter comes from the kitchen with an elegant bowl filled with steaming ... dirt soup.

This is not a joke, and it's not a nightmare, either. It's the start of an actual four-course meal at Ne Quittez Pas in Tokyo. The brainchild of chef Toshio Tanabe, the meal includes potato and soil soup, salad with dirt dressing, soil risotto with sautéed sea bass, and dirt ice cream for dessert. All of this can be had for the price of $110 per person.

While this might sound like a recipe for digestive disaster, reviewers have called the food "divine," and many say that it doesn't taste like dirt at all. This may be because Chef Tanabe uses only the finest dirt (and yes, there is such a thing!). Imported from Sri Lanka and India, the dirt is organic compost that's made from palm fiber and coffee grounds. It is rigorously tested for food safety.

For the chef, this is more than just a culinary stunt. He believes there are health benefits to eating soil. Though not all experts agree, some say that the bacteria in soil may help boost your immune system!

SURF AND SOIL RISOTTO

85

MUSICIAL FRUIT (AND VEGGIES)!

VIENNA, AUSTRIA

The Viennese Vegetable Orchestra may be the world's weirdest group of musicians. All of their instruments are carved out of vegetables and fruit! From pumpkin drums to celery guitars, each instrument is made fresh for each performance. Audiences enjoy the unique sounds of whistling carrot flutes, crackling onion skin, squawking red pepper horns, and more. At the end of some performances, fresh vegetable soup is served!

MAKE YOUR OWN WATERMELON DRUM

YOU'LL NEED:
1 HALF WATERMELON
1 MELON BALLER TOOL
1 CUTTING BOARD
2 CARROTS FOR DRUMSTICKS (OPTIONAL)

1. USE THE MELON BALLER TO SCRAPE THE FLESH OUT OF THE WATERMELON HALF.
2. TURN OVER THE WATERMELON AND PLACE IT FACEDOWN ON THE CUTTING BOARD.
3. PLAY YOUR WATERMELON DRU WITH CARROTS, YOUR HANDS, O THE MELON BALLER! SEE HOW YO CAN CHANGE THE SOUND BY LIFT ING THE EDGE OF THE MELON OF THE BOARD.

KOOL-AID
+PICKLES=
SWEET-AND-SOUR
SENSATION

SOUTHERN U.S.A.

It's hard to imagine thinking up the idea to put a packet of Kool-Aid mix in a pickle jar. But someone did exactly that—and now "Koolickles" are all the rage in the Mississippi Delta and other parts of the southern United States.

The pickles, which turn bright shades of red and green from soaking in the Kool-Aid, have a sweet-and-sour taste that is especially popular with kids. When the makers of Kool-Aid found out about this unusual invention, a company spokesperson told the *New York Times*, "We endorse our consumers' finding innovative ways to use our products." In other words, they think it's very kool!

MAKE YOUR OWN KOOLICKLES!

YOU'LL NEED:
- 1 HALF-GALLON (2-LITER) JAR OF PICKLES
- 1 EMPTY JAR OF SIMILAR SIZE
- 1 CUP SUGAR
- 1 PACKET UNSWEETENED KOOL-AID

1. DRAIN THE LIQUID FROM THE PICKLE JAR INTO THE EMPTY JAR.
2. ADD THE SUGAR AND THE KOOL-AID. STIR TO DISSOLVE.
3. POUR THE LIQUID MIXTURE BACK INTO THE JAR OF PICKLES. KEEP IN THE REFRIGERATOR FOR A WEEK, TURNING THE JAR ONCE PER DAY.

QUIZ

WHAT'S UP WITH THIS STRAWBERRY?
(SEE ANSWER BELOW)

A. IT FELL IN A BUCKET OF BLEACH.
B. IT'S THE GHOST OF A DEAD STRAWBERRY.
C. IT'S A NEW BREED OF STRAWBERRY THAT TASTES LIKE PINEAPPLE.

ANSWER: C! IT'S A PINEBERRY. DUTCH FARMERS FOUND A SAMPLE GROWING WILD IN SOUTH AMERICA. THEY TOOK IT HOME AND CULTI-VATED IT, CREATING THIS UNIQUE BREED. EACH PLANT PRODUCES ONLY A FEW PRECIOUS BERRIES, WHICH ARE POPULAR BUT EXPENSIV

CHAPTER 5

STRANGE
SCIENCE

JUMPING SPIDER HUNTS IN SPACE, PAGE 94

DINO-MITE GIRL

PINT-SIZE PALEONTOLOGIST!

ISLE OF WIGHT, ENGLAND

How would you like to have a dinosaur named after you? Paleontologists recently gave that honor to a girl named Daisy Morris. When Daisy was five years old, she discovered a dinosaur fossil while beachcombing with her family. When experts studied her fossil, they were amazed. The crow-size flying dinosaur is from a newly discovered species. Its name? *Vectidraco daisymorrisae*, or "Daisy-saurus." The fossil has been donated to the Natural History Museum in London.

TEST-TUBE BURGER

TRADITIONAL BURGER

WHO A DUTCH SCIENTIST AND THREE "TASTERS"

WHAT COOKED AND ATE HAMBURGER MEAT THAT WAS GROWN IN A LABORATORY

WHERE LONDON

HOW A TINY PIECE OF COW MUSCLE WAS USED TO GROW TENS OF BILLIONS OF HAMBURGER CELLS IN A LABORATORY. IT TOOK 20,000 CELLS OF THE LAB-GROWN MEAT TO FORM ONE BURGER. CREATING

ONE BURGER ALONE TOOK TWO YEARS AND COST $325,000!

WHY IT'S A WAY TO GROW MEAT WITHOUT WASTING PRECIOUS LAND, WATER, AND ENERGY. SCIENTISTS STILL HAVE TO FIGURE OUT HOW TO MAKE LAB MEAT TASTE AS GOOD AS REAL MEAT, THOUGH!

NEWS FEED

>>> **OSAKA UNIVERSITY, JAPAN:** RESEARCHERS HAVE CREATED MORE THAN A HUNDRED CHIRPING MICE IN ORDER TO STUDY LANGUAGE

PUPS PURSUE POOP

SUPER SNIFFER!

THREE FORKS, MONTANA, U.S.A.

A group called Working Dogs for Conservation trains dogs to be poop-sniffing specialists. The dogs have learned to detect the poop, or scat, of a wide range of threatened and endangered animals, including moon bears, gorillas, wolverines, and cheetahs. Working in rugged regions around the world, the canine detectives zero in on scat that humans might miss. Back in the lab, scientists analyze the scat to learn about a species' diet, health, and range.

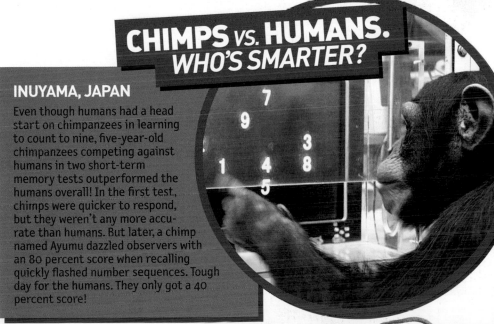

CHIMPS VS. HUMANS. WHO'S SMARTER?

INUYAMA, JAPAN

Even though humans had a head start on chimpanzees in learning to count to nine, five-year-old chimpanzees competing against humans in two short-term memory tests outperformed the humans overall! In the first test, chimps were quicker to respond, but they weren't any more accurate than humans. But later, a chimp named Ayumu dazzled observers with an 80 percent score when recalling quickly flashed number sequences. Tough day for the humans. They only got a 40 percent score!

COMMUNICATION. THE MICE CAN'T EXACTLY TALK LIKE MICKEY MOUSE, BUT THEY CAN TWEET LIKE TWEETY BIRD!

ASH CLOUD
CAUSES

VOLCANO GROUNDS
THOUSANDS OF PLANES

CHAOS!

EYJAFJALLAJÖKULL, ICELAND

WHEN THIS ICELANDIC VOLCANO BLEW ITS TOP IN 2010, air travel all over Europe was disrupted for nearly a week—with thousands of flights canceled. As if that mayhem wasn't enough, the raging volcano also generated its own lightning. Volcanic lightning happens when dust and rock particles collide as they shoot from the volcano, creating a static electric charge. *Crrrr-ack!*

OUT OF THIS WORLD!

JUMPING SPIDER
HUNTS IN SPACE

JUMPING SPIDERS CAN *SPRING* UP TO **50 TIMES** THEIR OWN **BODY LENGTHS** *TO CAPTURE PREY.*

INTERNATIONAL SPACE STATION, SPACE

What would happen if a jumping spider went to space? Could it still catch its prey while floating, when it tried to pounce?

This was the question that Egyptian teenager Amr Mohamed entered in a space-science contest. Mohamed won, so in 2012, a spider named Nefertiti was sent to live aboard the International Space Station for 100 days. The result? Nefertiti learned to sneak up next to her prey and grab it while clinging to her cage. When she returned to Earth, Nefertiti quickly readjusted and went right back to pouncing on her prey again. Score one for spider sense!

NEWS FEED

>>> **U.S.A.:** JUSTIN BIEBER IS READY FOR BLASTOFF! THE POP STAR PAID $250,000 TO BE AMONG THE FIRST PASSENGERS TO RIDE INTO SPACE ON VIRGIN

FLYING SAUCERS SPIN AROUND SATURN?

A YEAR ON SATURN LASTS LONGER THAN 29 EARTH YEARS.

SATURN, OUTER SPACE

Cool rings aren't Saturn's only claim to fame—it also has two weird moons that look like flying saucers! Called Pan and Atlas, the two moons orbit within the planet's rings. Scientists have known about the moons since the early 1980s, but it wasn't until recently, when the Cassini spacecraft took new photos, that the moons' shapes were fully revealed.

How did Saturn end up with such strange moons? Scientists believe that the particles of rock found in the planet's rings stuck to Pan and Atlas, forming the thick ridge that appears around each moon's equator.

THE KEPLER SPACE TELESCOPE HAS DETECTED STARS SOME 3,000 LIGHT-YEARS AWAY FROM EARTH.

EARTH'S LONG-LOST TWINS?

ACROSS THE GALAXY

Hoping to find other life in the universe, scientists on NASA's Kepler mission have been combing outer space for a planet just like home. In April 2013 they had their biggest breakthrough yet, when they discovered not one but two "Earth twins" orbiting a star called Kepler-62.

The newfound planets are similar in size to Earth, and they're both the right distance from the star to be habitable and for water (if there is any) to be liquid. So, when can we visit? Not soon, unfortunately. The trip would take 1,200 years if we could travel at the speed of light!

GALACTIC'S *SPACESHIPTWO*, A ROCKET-POWERED VEHICLE FUNDED BY THE OWNER OF VIRGIN ATLANTIC AIRWAYS.

MOVE OVER, SKYSCRAPER,

MEET THE STRAWSCRAPER!

STOCKHOLM, SWEDEN

For some people, a windy day is a bad hair day. But for the folks designing this odd-looking building, a windy day is a good hair day. For them, windy days will mean the hairy fibers on their building are capturing loads of free energy!

A Swedish architectural firm is working on plans to transform an existing Stockholm building into a futuristic 40-floor skyscraper that will create energy. The design for this project, known as the Strawscraper, encloses the building in a casing covered with long, flexible straws that turn wind motion into electrical energy. Whether the weather forecast calls for strong winds or gentle breezes, the friction on the straws will produce and store electricity much like a wind power plant does. The Strawscraper will be much quieter than wind turbine energy, though, and it will be bird-friendly, too. (Birds sometimes fly into the blades of wind turbines.)

Although still in the planning stages, it's clear that the Strawscraper—shown here in concept form—will stand out. As the fringe whips in the wind, this "hairway" to heaven will seem to be a living, breathing thing!

WIND ENERGY *IN THE U.S.* COULD POWER THE COUNTRY **10 TIMES** OVER.

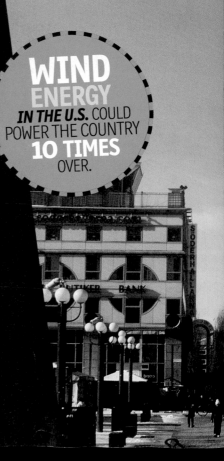

IMAGING THE
VIEW FROM THE TOP

WINDMILLS
HAVE BEEN USED
FOR **MORE THAN**
4,000
YEARS.

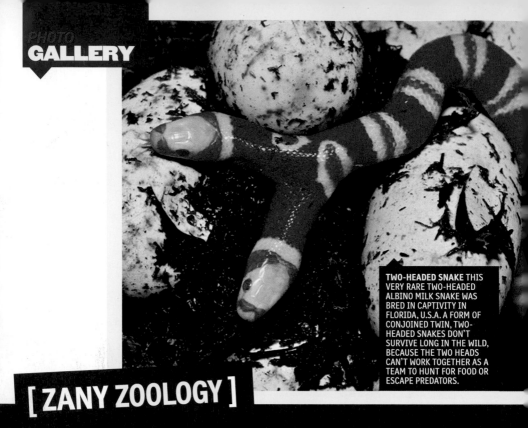

TWO-HEADED SNAKE THIS VERY RARE TWO-HEADED ALBINO MILK SNAKE WAS BRED IN CAPTIVITY IN FLORIDA, U.S.A. A FORM OF CONJOINED TWIN, TWO-HEADED SNAKES DON'T SURVIVE LONG IN THE WILD, BECAUSE THE TWO HEADS CAN'T WORK TOGETHER AS A TEAM TO HUNT FOR FOOD OR ESCAPE PREDATORS.

[ZANY ZOOLOGY]

This crazy collection of rare breeds and genetic oddities from around the globe just might make you do a double take!

WORLD'S HEAVIEST INSECT A SCIENTIST DISCOVERED THE WORLD'S HEAVIEST INSECT ON A TINY ISLAND IN NEW ZEALAND—AND FED IT A CARROT! AT 2.5 OUNCES (71 G), THIS GIANT WETA IS THREE TIMES HEAVIER THAN A MOUSE.

WETAS
HAVE **BEEN** **AROUND** SINCE **BEFORE** THE **DINOSAURS.**

SMALL SNEAKY SPIDERS A SMALL SPIDER DISCOVERED IN PERU'S AMAZON RAIN FOREST WEAVES LARGE DECOYS OF MUCH BIGGER SPIDERS INTO ITS WEBS TO MAKE PREDATORS THINK A BIG SCARY SPIDER LIVES THERE! FOOLED YA!

THE **GOLIATH** BIRD-EATING SPIDER GOT ITS NAME AFTER AN EXPLORER SAW ONE EAT A HUMMINGBIRD.

GLOW-IN-THE-DARK PIGLETS NOT ALL ADAPTATIONS HAPPEN NATURALLY. THESE PIGLETS GLOW IN THE DARK BECAUSE SCIENTISTS INSERTED GLOWING JELLYFISH DNA INTO THEIR GENES. THOUGH ANIMAL-RIGHTS QUESTIONS HAVE BEEN RAISED ABOUT THE PRACTICE, THIS KIND OF RESEARCH CAN HELP SCIENTISTS BETTER UNDERSTAND HOW GENES WORK.

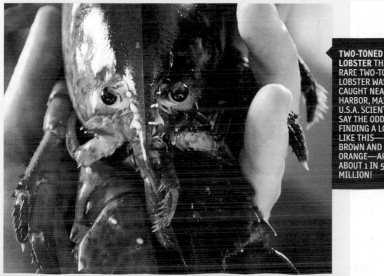

TWO-TONED LOBSTER THIS RARE TWO-TONED LOBSTER WAS CAUGHT NEAR BAR HARBOR, MAINE, U.S.A. SCIENTISTS SAY THE ODDS OF FINDING A LOBSTER LIKE THIS—HALF BROWN AND HALF ORANGE—ARE ABOUT 1 IN 50 MILLION!

CLOUDY

THE NETHERLANDS

WHO LET THAT CLOUD IN? Dutch artist Berndnaut Smilde blends science and art to create indoor clouds that look just like real ones. By carefully controlling the temperature and keeping the air moist, Smilde uses a fog machine to produce a single puffy cloud that hovers in midair. With artful lighting, he can even mimic the glow of sunlight shining through the mist! These artificial clouds don't last long, though—just long enough to snap a picture!

WITH A CHANCE OF
ARt

POLLY WANT A Ph.D.?

BIRD BRAINS

CARRION CROWS WILL PLACE **WALNUTS** IN THE **ROAD** SO CARS **RUN OVER** THEM AND THE CROWS CAN GET A **TASTY TREAT.**

RAVENS USE THEIR **BEAKS** AND **WINGS** TO **POINT TO OBJECTS,** JUST LIKE WE USE **OUR HANDS.**

ALEX THE PARROT
ACES MATH

BRIGHT BIRD
WOWS THE WORLD

MASSACHUSETTS, U.S.A.

Thanks to an African gray parrot named Alex, being called a "birdbrain" can actually be a compliment! Alex learned to speak more than 120 words and to identify colors, shapes, and numbers. But that's not all—as recently published research has shown, Alex could do math, too.

The bird was trained by scientist Irene Pepperberg using an innovative method. Since parrots are social animals, Pepperberg had a second trainer play the part of Alex's fellow student and rival. Alex would watch as his rival spoke a new word when shown a new object—a grape, for example—and was rewarded with that object. To get the new object for himself, Alex learned the word.

Pepperberg began to realize that Alex could do math, as well, when he showed he could count objects. For example, if Alex was shown a tray of blocks of different colors—four green, three red, and five blue—and asked, "What color five?" Alex would respond "blue."

This smart parrot went on to show that he could accurately add two sets of objects, as long as the sum was six or fewer. In Pepperberg's final experiments, Alex showed he could also add two numbers, even beyond a total of six, demonstrating that 3 + 4 = 7, and 4 + 4 = 8. Now that's worth a grape for sure!

DOG LEARNS MORE THAN 1,000 WORDS

SPARTANBURG, SOUTH CAROLINA, U.S.A.

Meet Chaser, a border collie known as the "most scientifically important dog in more than a century." Chaser's owner, psychology professor John Pilley, used his animal-learning expertise to teach Chaser one or two new words a day. Pilley spent hours repeating names of new toys to Chaser, and then they'd play hide-and-seek with the objects. Chaser loved the drills so much that within three years she could identify 800 different cloth animals, 116 balls, and 26 Frisbees.

SECRET SLEUTH

WHO HEATHER DEWEY-HAGBORG, AN ARTIST WHO'S INTERESTED IN THE SCIENCE OF CRIME SOLVING

WHAT USES PEOPLE'S DNA SHE FINDS IN PUBLIC PLACES TO MAKE PORTRAITS OF WHAT THE OWNERS MIGHT LOOK LIKE

WHERE NEW YORK CITY, NEW YORK, U.S.A.

HOW SHE MAKES 3-D COMPUTER-PRINTED IMAGES USING DNA FROM DISCARDED CHEWING GUM, HAIR STRANDS, AND CIGARETTES.

WHY TO HELP US REALIZE HOW THE TRACES WE LEAVE BEHIND CAN BE USED TO LEARN SOMETHING ABOUT US.

NEWS FEED

>>> **RALEIGH, NORTH CAROLINA, U.S.A.:** SCIENTISTS AT NORTH CAROLINA STATE UNIVERSITY EXAMINED LINT SAMPLES FROM 60 PEOPLE'S NAVELS.

A MAMMOTH DISCOVERY

SIBERIA, RUSSIA

A 10,000-year-old woolly mammoth's body was recently found buried underground, preserved in ice. When scientists dug it out, they were excited to find a dark liquid in the massive beast's carcass. If, in fact, the fluid contains the animal's DNA, could it be used to re-create extinct mammoths? Cloning in a science lab is probably impossible if the cells are too damaged, but it's fun to imagine bringing this ancient elephant-like creature back to life!

MAMMOTH MUMMY!

SARASOTA BAY, FLORIDA, U.S.A.

"Hey, Flipper, where are you?" Bottlenose dolphins have names for themselves and each other. But instead of using words to communicate, like we do, they use whistle sounds. When one dolphin is looking for a friend, it mimics his buddy's whistle sound as a way of saying: "I'm looking for you." They're the only animals (other than humans) known to communicate like this.

DOLPHINS CALL EACH OTHER BY NAME—WITH WHISTLE SIGNATURES!

Q-TIP SWABS PICKED UP 2,368 BACTERIAL SPECIES, MANY OF WHICH HAD NEVER BEEN SEEN BEFORE!

PHYSICIST INVENTS A REAL HAIR-RAISER

A star attraction at science museums around the world can electrify you! Physicist Robert Van de Graaff invented a generator in 1931 that was used as a power supply for the world's earliest particle accelerators. (Particle accelerators speed up atoms and smash them together.) The Van de Graaff generator that you can touch in a museum is less high-powered but it works on the same principles. It generates static electricity that gives your hair strands a positive charge. Since things with the same charge repel one another, your hair strands spread out and away from your head!

1931

>>> MAD SCIENCE IN THE 20TH CENTURY

1971

ASTRONAUT DROPS HAMMER AND FEATHER ON MOON

Hammer or feather: Which falls fastest? In 1971 Apollo 15 Commander David Scott took a moment from his moonwalk to demonstrate proof of the theory—first established by Galileo—that objects fall at the same rate regardless of mass. On Earth, a feather falls more slowly than a hammer because of air resistance, but the moon has almost no atmosphere, so the feather and the hammer landed at the same time. Surely Galileo never dreamed that his theory would someday be proven on the moon!

CHIMPS GRUNT WHEN HAPPY.

MELTED CHOCOLATE LEADS TO MAJOR DISCOVERY

BABY CHIMP RAISED WITH BABY HUMAN

1931

To help test the theory that a chimpanzee raised alongside a human baby would learn to talk and act like a human, in 1931 psychologist Winthrop Kellogg brought home a seven-month-old chimp named Gua. The plan was for Gua to grow up alongside Kellogg's own ten-month-old son, Donald. The outcome? Gua didn't learn to speak or act like a human. Donald, on the other hand, started grunting and biting like a chimp! Kellogg had no choice but to abandon the experiment.

1946

Ever wonder how the microwave came to be? In 1946, just after World War II, engineer Percy LeBaron Spencer was working at a company that made magnetrons for radar systems. (Magnetrons produce microwaves, a type of electromagnetic wave.) Working near a magnetron, Spencer was surprised to discover that the chocolate bar in his pocket had melted. The engineer went on to test popcorn (it popped), and an egg (it exploded). The microwave oven was born!

ELEVEN MEN SIGN UP TO SPEND A YEAR IN BED

1986

PEOPLE CAN TAKE CATNAPS WITH THEIR EYES OPEN.

What do you think it would be like to spend 370 days in bed? In 1986 Soviet space-travel researchers recruited 11 men to do just that. Why? Lying down has a similar effect on the body to weightlessness in space, since the heart, muscles, and bones don't have to work very hard. The men ate, washed, read, and watched TV in their beds. Tensions ran high (and one guy dropped out). The takeaway? Scientists realized that long-term space travel would be as hard on the mind as it would be on the body!

NAME THAT WEIRD DISCOVERY!

Each of these pictures captures a strange new revelation from the world of science. Look at each picture and see if you can figure out which of the three choices is the REAL weird but true discovery! The answers are at the bottom of page 109.

1. WHAT'S THE SCOOP?

A. Prehistoric potatoes were 20 times bigger than today's potatoes.
B. Ancient clay balls suggest that Neanderthal children enjoyed arts and crafts.
C. Piles of fossilized poo may show that dinosaurs pooped in special toilet areas.

2. WHAT DOES THIS IMAGE REVEAL?

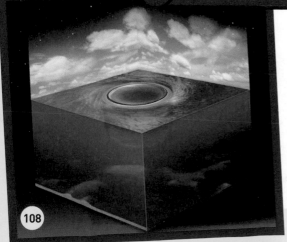

A. A mysterious island with a red lagoon in the Pacific Ocean is really an ancient landing pad.
B. Earth's oceans have whirlpools that are similar to black holes.
C. Earth is really rectangular.

3. WHAT'S THE *REAL* DISCOVERY?

A. Ancient statues were possibly *walked* to their locations by teams of people using ropes.
B. Statues are easiest to topple when they're blindfolded.
C. Ancient people used to play a game like tug-of-war with a statue in the middle.

4. WHAT'S THE CONNECTION HERE?

A. Tests show that male jaguars prefer men's cologne to women's perfume.
B. Biologists discover jaguars can be lured by the smell of a popular men's cologne.
C. In a smell test, the majority of women associate popular men's cologne with jaguars.

5. THIS IS A MICROSCOPIC VIEW OF ...

A. Two different kinds of frost on a car window.
B. Two different kinds of dried human tears, from grief and onions.
C. Life on Mars!

ANSWERS: 1.C; 2.B; 3.A; 4.B; 5.B

109

CHAPTER 6

WAY-OUT
TRAVEL

K A FLIGHT • SLEEP TIGHT • ONE-WAY TICKET TO
STINATION • FIRST PERSON TO TRAVEL AROUND
LYING • SPACE SHUTTLE: STUCK IN TRAFFIC • PA
MANSION ON WHEELS • HEADS UP! • A
DINING UNDER THE

TOUR TOKYO IN ONE WACKY DAY, PAGE 124

SPACED OUT

BOOK A FLIGHT

NEW MEXICO, U.S.A.

When thinking of your next vacation, add outer space to the list. Perhaps as early as 2014, you won't need to be a real astronaut for an out-of-this-world adventure. Several private companies are geared up to train citizens on the basics of spaceflight in preparation for a zero-gravity experience. But these luxury trips are not cheap. For a seat on the Virgin Galactic VSS Enterprise—including your space suit—you'll spend $250,000.

A **HUMAN** CAN **SURVIVE** (UNPROTECTED) **IN SPACE** FOR ONLY **2** MINUTES!

NEWS FEED
>>> **SPACE:** SPACE STINKS! SO SAY ASTRONAUTS RETURNING FROM SPACE WALKS. WHEN THEY GET BACK TO THE SPACE STATION AND TAKE OFF THEIR HELMETS,

SLEEP TIGHT

LAS VEGAS, NEVADA, U.S.A.

Ever wonder where you'd stay on your space vacation? Not to worry. Plans are in the works for the first space station for regular space travelers. Guests can expect to pay more than $25 million for a 30-day stay on the Sundancer space station. The hefty price tag includes space transportation, all supplies, and astronaut training. Crews will periodically dock next to the space capsule to deliver supply refills. It's safe to say that visitors will be getting some shut-eye farther from home than they had ever ventured before!

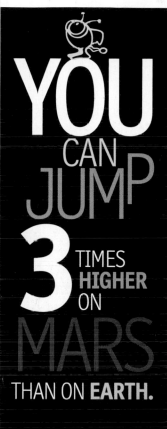

YOU CAN JUMP 3 TIMES HIGHER ON MARS THAN ON EARTH.

ONE-WAY TICKET TO MARS

NETHERLANDS

A Dutch company called Mars One is hoping some hard-core space travelers will wish to stay in space for good! They are expecting to form a human colony on Mars by 2023. But people who sign up are only allowed a one-way ticket. Not only does this keep the cost of the flight down, but changes in atmosphere and gravity will affect the human body so much that the new Mars colonists would not be able to live on Earth again. The fearless colonists will eat mostly dried or canned foods, and get some of their water from recycled urine!

THEY SMELL ODD ODORS LIKE COOKED STEAK AND HOT METAL. SCIENTISTS SAY THE AROMAS ARE CAUSED BY PARTICLES THE ASTRONAUTS BRING BACK INSIDE.

THE SWEETEST DESTINATiON

NEW YORK CITY, NEW YORK, U.S.A.

IMAGINE SPENDING THE NIGHT in a hotel room made of chocolate! That's the delectable prize snagged by the lucky winner of a Valentine's Day giveaway promotion by world-famous chocolatier Godiva in 2008. The sweet suite was created in New York's Bryant Park Hotel. The walls, chandeliers, paintings, and beds were made of chocolate, or at least covered in the sugary treat. The items that couldn't be made of chocolate were painted to look like chocolate. Take that, sweet tooth!

FIRST PERSON
TO TRAVEL
AROUND WORLD
WITHOUT
FLYING

LIVEPOOL, ENGLAND

British adventurer Graham Hughes took the challenge of a lifetime when he decided to visit every organized nation in the world—without hopping on a plane. Traveling by foot, taxi, bus, train, ship, and even canoe, Hughes made 201 international border crossings. During the 1,426-day trip, which ended on November 26, 2012, he filled four passport books with stamps from border agents.

SPACE SHUTTLE:
STUCK IN TRAFFIC

WHAT THE SPACE SHUTTLE *ENDEAVOUR* TRAVELED BY ROAD TO ITS NEW HOME, A SCIENCE CENTER.

WHEN OCTOBER 2012

WHERE LOS ANGELES, CALIFORNIA, U.S.A. AFTER ARRIVING AT LOS ANGELES INTERNATIONAL AIRPORT ON THE BACK OF A 747 AIRCRAFT, *ENDEAVOUR* JOURNEYED 12 MILES (19 KM) TO THE CALIFORNIA SCIENCE CENTER.

HOW PERCHED ATOP A 160-WHEELED CARRIER, *ENDEAVOUR* INCHED THROUGH STREETS AT 2 MILES (3.2 KM) AN HOUR. FREQUENT STOPS WERE MADE TO CHECK *ENDEAVOUR*'S BALANCE AND PRUNE TREES BLOCKING ITS PATH. THE TRIP TOOK TWO DAYS.

WHY AFTER 30 YEARS OF SPACE-FLIGHTS, *ENDEAVOUR* WAS READY FOR RETIREMENT. THE SHUTTLE IS NOW A TOP ATTRACTION AT THE SCIENCE CENTER.

NEWS FEED

>>> **ICELAND:** AFTER AMERICAN TOURISTS SET UP A TABLE AND CHAIRS FOR A PICNIC ON AN ICELANDIC GLACIER, THEIR SECTION OF THE ICEBERG

PARROT THIEF *TARGETS* TOURIST

SOUTH ISLAND, NEW ZEALAND

Scottish tourist Peter Leach got more than he bargained for when he stopped his camper van in Arthur's Pass National Park to take a picture of a species of parrot called a kea. While Leach was sightseeing, the bird snatched about $1,000 of local currency from inside Leach's van. It wasn't the first kea caper. A few years earlier, another Scottish tourist had his passport stolen by a kea!

MANSION ON WHEELS

AUSTRIA

Behold the eleMMent Palazzo, a $3 million vacation home on wheels. Austrian company Marchi Mobile designed the luxury vehicle with the wealthiest campers in mind. The 40-foot (12-m)-long camper comes complete with skylights, a leather interior, master bedroom with private bathroom, fireplace, and 40-inch (102-cm) television.

BROKE FREE. THEY FLOATED ABOUT 32 FEET (10 M) OUT TO SEA BEFORE THEY WERE RESCUED.

OPEN YOUR OWN HOTEL ROOM ANYWHERE YOU ARE AND THEN FOLD IT UP AND TAKE IT WITH YOU WHEN YOU'RE DONE.

[GEAR & GADGET GUIDE]

No one likes to travel unprepared for life's little challenges. This guide of gear and gadgets for the offbeat traveler and adventurer might leave you wondering, *Now, why didn't I think of that?*

SEARCHING FOR ALIENS? THIS NOVELTY UFO DETECTOR WILL ADD TO YOUR FUN. BEEPS AND FLASHES ALERT YOU TO ELECTROMAGNETIC DISTURBANCES IN THE AREA. THE REST IS UP TO YOU!

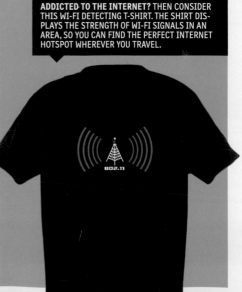

ADDICTED TO THE INTERNET? THEN CONSIDER THIS WI-FI DETECTING T-SHIRT. THE SHIRT DISPLAYS THE STRENGTH OF WI-FI SIGNALS IN AN AREA, SO YOU CAN FIND THE PERFECT INTERNET HOTSPOT WHEREVER YOU TRAVEL.

OSTRICHES PRESS THEIR HEADS AND NECKS TO THE GROUND WHEN SLEEPiNG.

SOMETIMES TRAVELING MAKES YOU WANT TO BURY YOUR HEAD IN THE SAND. THAT'S WHERE THE OSTRICH PILLOW CAN COME IN HANDY. STAY COMFY, HIDE FROM THE WORLD, AND CATCH SOME ZZZZ'S.

YOU WON'T MISS THE BEAUTIFUL SCENERY AROUND YOU WHILE YOU CAMP IN THE COMFORT OF YOUR SEE-THROUGH BUBBLE TENT. CHECK OUT THE FURNITURE AND ELECTRIC LIGHTING!

HEADS UP!

ST. MAARTEN

TOURISTS ENJOYING THE SUN, sand, and surf at Maho Beach on the Caribbean island of St. Maarten get more than a great suntan. They also get a spectacular show of giant jet planes flying overhead—very low overhead! The planes are on their way to landing at the Princess Juliana International Airport just next door. Ever since photos of the low-flying planes were first publicized, the beach has been the ultimate travel destination for plane spotters. They can check the flight schedule and plan their day around the sight of huge jets landing on the short, 7,150-foot (2,180-m) runway. Where else can people welcome the island's newest tourists while working on their tan?

UNDERWATER EXPLORER!

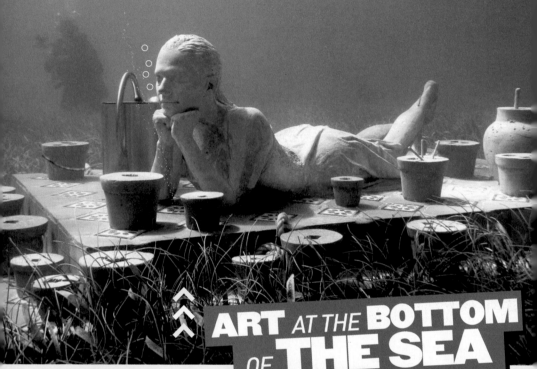

ART *AT THE* BOTTOM *OF* THE SEA

CANCÚN, MEXICO

After hurricanes and storms damaged Cancún's natural coral reefs, artists and conservationists put their heads together to think of a way to help the reef recover. Their solution? An underwater museum! They lowered sculptures to a nearby area that would serve as an artificial reef for animals to inhabit. At the same time, the attraction led divers away from the recovering natural reef and into an amazing underwater world. Today the museum has some 460 sculptures, and the natural coral reefs are slowly being restored.

YOUR **HEART RATE** IS *SLOWER* IN WATER THAN IN THE AIR.

NEWS FEED

>>> **HAWAII, U.S.A., AND TAIWAN:** IN 2007 A WOMAN IN HAWAII LOST HER UNDERWATER CAMERA ON A DIVING TRIP. IN FEBRUARY 2013 THE CAMERA WASHED

MALDIVES, ASIA

Feeling like some seafood? That's the specialty cuisine at Ithaa restaurant, the world's first all-glass underwater restaurant, open since 2005. To get there, simply walk into a thatched roof pavilion at the end of a pier, and descend 16 feet (5 m) down a spiral staircase through an underwater tunnel. While you're dining below the waves, you can take in 180-degree views of beautiful coral gardens and schools of fish gliding through the Indian Ocean. But make reservations at Conrad Maldives Rangali Island Hotel well ahead of time —this restaurant seats only 12 diners at a time. And don't be surprised if the fish gaze at your plate and wonder what you're eating!

DINING UNDER
THE WAVES

WATER SPIDERS LIVE UNDERWATER BY BREATHING AIR THEY TRAP AT THE SURFACE.

SUNKEN TOWN
COMES UP FOR AIR

EPECUÉN, ARGENTINA

Years ago, people visited this charming lakeside resort town near Buenos Aires for its relaxing saltwater baths and spas. Then in 1985 heavy rains and flooding caused the whole town to be submerged in nearly 30 feet (9 m) of salt water. Some thought the town was gone forever. But since 2009 the floodwaters have been receding. Now the town is back on the map—and tourists come for another reason. The amazing effects of years of corrosive salt water have made the village look like a creepy ghost town.

UP ON A BEACH IN TAIWAN. THE MEMORY CARD HELPED TO IDENTIFY THE OWNER AND THE CAMERA WAS RETURNED. BETTER LATE THAN NEVER!

IN TOKYO,
A CHEF CUT A
SINGLE PIECE OF HAM THAT STRETCHED
AS LONG AS A
SCHOOL BUS.

TOKYO, JAPAN

Tokyo, the capital of Japan, is the largest metropolitan area in the world. The city is known for mixing the ancient with the ultramodern, with temples dating to the seventh century just blocks from brand-new skyscrapers and mesmerizing city lights. The city even claims the world's busiest pedestrian crosswalk, Shibuya Crossing, with over a million people scurrying across it daily.

MORNING

If you're into quirky sightseeing, check out this one-day tour of Tokyo's finest wacky attractions. Just getting there is half the fun. The city is so crowded, the subway system has "SUBWAY STUFFERS," assigned the task of gently pushing the riders into the train cars so the doors will close.

While in town, check out Tokyo's local parks, where fashion never sleeps. Here you'll get a glimpse of young people called "TRIBES," or "KEI." They display eye-popping fashion trends, hoping to outshine competing tribes.

THE **SHINJUKU RAILWAY STATION** HAS MORE THAN **200** EXITS.

TOKYO
IN ONE WACKY DAY

NIGHTTIME

At the end of the day, get cozy for the night in a room the size of a dog kennel at one of Tokyo's **CAPSULE HOTELS.**

LUNCH

Next stop, lunch! Visit a **CAT CAFÉ** where you can play with cats during your meal. Then, try a **COMIC BOOK CAFÉ** where you get your own private booth for hours of comic book reading.

AFTERNOON

After lunch, visit an amusement park with a 60-foot (18-m), 39-ton (35-mT) **GUNDAM ROBOT** standing guard outside. If that's too much excitement for you, visit a library made of bookshelves instead of bricks at the Musashino Art University.

125

SALAR DE UYUNI, BOLIVIA PILES OF SALT READY FOR TRANSPORT DOT THE WORLD'S LARGEST SALT FLAT. WHEN COVERED IN RAINWATER, THE FLATS BECOME A MIRROR, MAKING VISITORS APPEAR TO BE WALKING ON CLOUDS. TOURISTS FLOCK HERE TO OBSERVE THE UNIQUE LANDSCAPE—AND REFLECT!

[MAGICAL MYSTERY TOUR]

If you're a traveler in search of life's mysteries, here are some places around the world that will make you wonder, *Why does that happen?* Or, *How did they do that?* Don't forget your detective hat when you visit these top five mysterious places and spaces.

SPLIT APPLE ROCK, NEW ZEALAND WHAT MADE THIS ROUND BOULDER SPLIT PERFECTLY DOWN THE MIDDLE? NO ONE KNOWS, BUT IT'S A FUN AND POPULAR TOURIST DESTINATION IN ABEL TASMAN NATIONAL PARK ON NEW ZEALAND'S SOUTH ISLAND. VISITORS CAN ALSO HIKE, CAMP, KAYAK, AND SWIM NEAR THE MYSTERY ROCK.

SAILING STONES, RACETRACK PLAYA, U.S.A. IN DEATH VALLEY, WHERE ABOUT A MILLION TOURISTS A YEAR VISIT, STONES "SAIL" ACROSS THE DRY, CRACKED EARTH ALL BY THEMSELVES. RECENT THEORIES SUGGEST A THIN LAYER OF ICE UNDER THE ROCKS MAY CAUSE THE MOVEMENT, BUT IT STILL LEAVES VISITORS FLABBERGASTED.

SOME JARS

AT THE

PLAIN OF JARS

ARE AS TALL AS A **1-STORY BUILDING.**

MOUNT RORAIMA, SOUTH AMERICA ONE OF EARTH'S OLDEST LAND FORMATIONS, THIS MOUNTAIN ALMOST ALWAYS HAS CLOUDS BELOW ITS FLAT TOP. SOME PLANTS AND ANIMALS HERE ARE FOUND NOWHERE ELSE ON EARTH.

PLAIN OF JARS, LAOS THIS GIANT CLUSTER OF STONE CYLINDERS, OR JARS, HAS BEEN SITTING HERE FOR MORE THAN 2,000 YEARS. ARCHAEOLOGISTS HAVE LITTLE IDEA OF THE ANCIENT PEOPLE WHO MADE THE JARS. BUT TODAY, HUNDREDS OF TOURISTS BOOK TRIPS TO THE SITE. MAYBE SOMEDAY ONE OF THEM WILL SOLVE THE MYSTERY OF THESE ODD JARS.

WHERE IN THE
WORLD?

IMAGINE YOU WAKE UP each morning in a different, mystery location around the world. You might be on any of the world's continents. Use the map to help you locate seven weird but true vacation spots. The clues here will help you decide ... Where in the world am I?

(The answers are at bottom.)

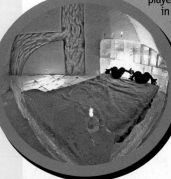

① LEPRECHAUN MUSEUM

You're visiting a national leprechaun museum with oversize furniture that makes you the leprechaun. When the museum opened in 2010, the museum's designer pointed out that the furniture had the correct "human-to-leprechaun proportions." Where in the world are you? Name the country and the continent and find your place on the map.

② ICE HOTEL

This place is cold enough for an ice hotel, but the folks here (including the professional hockey players) don't typically live in igloos. Where in the world are you? Name the country and the continent.

③ LANGATA GIRAFFE CENTRE

You're in the Giraffe Centre, a nature preserve for Rothschild giraffes, an endangered species. You're allowed to walk free with these beautiful creatures, and even feed them from your hand or kiss them. The preserve is in a suburb just outside the capital city of Nairobi. Where in the world are you? Name the country and the continent.

④ ELEPHANT NATURE PARK

You're at a rescue center where you are allowed to play with, ride, and bathe elephants. And you're not too far from the city of Chiang Mai, where you can get a great dish of pad thai for dinner. Where in the world are you? Name the country and the continent.

ANSWERS: 1. C-Ireland, Europe; 2. E-Canada, North America; 3. B-Kenya, Africa; 4. A-Thailand, Asia; 5. G-Australia; 6. F-Brazil, South America; 7. D-Antarctica

Arctic Ocean

E

C

Atlantic
Ocean

Pacific
Ocean

A

B

F

Indian
Ocean

acific
Ocean

G

D

6 RAIN FOREST PARROT

You're on a birding
tour through the misty
Amazon rain forest and
you spot a colorful
parrot among other
amazing bird species.
Tours occur in other
countries on the
continent, such as
Ecuador and Venezuela,
but the Amazon runs
through more of this
country than through
any other. Where in the
world are you? Name
the country and the
continent.

5 KANGAROO

You're on a safari to
see wild animals, but
you're nowhere near
the usual safari
animals. Instead, you
see wallabies, koalas,
and kangaroos. In
fact, you're on the
country's third
largest island, called
Kangaroo Island.
Where in the world
are you? Name
the country and
the continent.

7 RESEARCH STATION

You're on a continent
that has no countries
in it! However, seven
countries have
claimed areas of the
icy continent, mostly
for scientific research
stations like this one.
Where in the world
are you?

CHAPTER 7

WEIRD
WORLD OF SPORTS

FLORA
28291
adidas
WaterAid
Water for life

WaterAid

WaterAid

WACKY RECORDS — SHATTERED! PAGE 148

BIKER VS. FALCON IN DOWNHILL RACE

WALES

Who's the fastest downhill racer—bike or bird? Mountain biking champ Gee Atherton got in gear to answer that question. He strapped some bird bait to his back and a camera to his helmet. Then he bolted down a twisting mountain trail. "It was really hard to concentrate knowing the falcon's razor-sharp talons were just centimeters from my head," admitted Atherton. The falcon stayed close to the biker most of the way down, then finally grabbed the loot and won the race. Don't mess with the falcon!

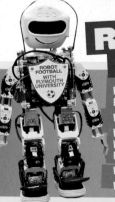

ROBOTS COMPETE FOR ROBOWORLD CUP

WHO FEDERATION OF INTERNATIONAL ROBOT-SOCCER ASSOCIATION

WHAT ROBOWORLD CUP

WHERE KUALA LUMPUR, MALAYSIA, WITH 80 TEAMS FROM 11 COUNTRIES PARTICIPATING

WHEN AUGUST 2013

WHY SINCE 1996, THE WORLD'S TECH-IEST ROBOT ATHLETES HAVE BEEN COMPETING IN SOCCER, WEIGHT LIFTING, BASKETBALL, AND SPRINTING. THESE METAL MARVELS IMPROVE EACH YEAR. THE LATEST WEIGHT-LIFTING BOTS LIFT UPWARDS OF 100 DVDS OVER THEIR HEADS. AND HUMANS CHEER THEM ON FROM THE SIDELINES.

NEWS FEED

>>> PHILADELPHIA, PENNSYLVANIA, U.S.A.: COULD IT BE SUPERSTITION THAT LED WASHINGTON NATIONALS SHORTSTOP IAN DESMOND TO SHAVE

TOILET
DOUBLES AS SOCCER GOALIE

JAPAN

Two Japanese companies put their heads together to come up with the latest in soccer technology—a toilet goalie. But the S.G.T.K. (Super Great Toilet Keeper) is not your average toilet. In just 0.1 second, two high-speed cameras on the toilet capture the destination of a soccer ball that has been kicked toward it. The toilet then adjusts its position and shoots out a smaller ball, knocking the soccer ball away from the goal. And it always puts the lid down when it's finished!

SHARK
FALLS FROM SKY ONTO GOLF COURSE

SAN JUAN CAPISTRANO, CALIFORNIA, U.S.A.

What would you do if, say, you saw a shark fall from the sky? Grab a friend, put the shark in a bucket of homemade salt water, and return it to the nearby ocean, of course! That's exactly what one golf course employee did while he was inspecting the lush greens of a golf course in San Juan Capistrano. Authorities say the two-foot (60-cm)-long leopard shark must have fallen out of the grips of a feisty bird of prey while it was flying overhead.

OFF HIS GOATEE BETWEEN INNINGS OF A TOUGH GAME WITH THE PHILADELPHIA PHILLIES ON JULY 9, 2013—THEN HEAD BACK ONTO THE FIELD FOR A FRESH START?

133

MUGGLES PLAY IN
QUIDDITCH

SO FAR, NO ONE HAS TAKEN OFF ON A BROOMSTICK IN THE QUIDDITCH WORLD CUP GAMES.

KISSIMMEE, FLORIDA, U.S.A.

Who says only wizards can play Quidditch? Once upon a time, it was just an imaginary game in J. K. Rowling's Harry Potter books. But now, Muggles, or nonwizards, can compete in the game—up to the World Cup level.

Quidditch in the real world was the brainchild of Xander Manshel, a freshman at a Vermont college in 2005. The first group of players wore towels as capes. And since they could not really fly, they chose any broom they could find. Some brought mops. One student even used a floor lamp from his dorm room.

The rules of play are mainly based on the game as described in the Harry Potter books. It's part lacrosse, a touch of rugby, and a little bit of dodgeball wrapped up in one.

The game spread fast. Quidditch is now played in more than 1,000 colleges and high schools throughout North America, Australia, and Europe—and there's also an International Quidditch Association. But no one has yet reported a player taking off on a broomstick!

WORLD CUP

LACROSSE STICKS DOUBLE AS BROOMSTICKS FOR FLIGHTLESS QUIDDITCH PLAYERS.

WHEN FICTION COMES TO LIFE: HARRY POTTER WAS A "SEEKER" FOR THE GRYFFINDOR TEAM. NOW REAL STUDENTS CAN CATCH THE GOLDEN SNITCH.

CRAZY
COLLECTIBLES

KING OF ALL CARDS

FIRST BASEMAN GETS WORLD'S LARGEST BASEBALL CARD

LAKELAND, FLORIDA, U.S.A.

Most of the time you can fit a baseball card in your back pocket. But not so with a 90-foot (27-m)-long, 60-foot (18-m)-wide baseball card of Detroit Tigers first baseman Prince Fielder. Unveiled in 2013, the world's largest baseball card covered most of center field at Peterson Park, near the Tigers' spring training camp in Florida. It would take 82,944 regular-size baseball cards to cover the surface of this massive piece of memorabilia. Try trading that one!

THE WORLD'S MOST EXPENSIVE **BASEBALL CARD**—A *1909* **HONUS WAGNER** —SOLD FOR **$2.8 MILLION** IN 2007.

NEWS FEED

>>> **NEW YORK CITY, NEW YORK, U.S.A.:** LEGENDARY OUTFIELDER TY COBB'S CONTRIBUTIONS TO PRO BASEBALL IN THE EARLY 20TH CENTURY MADE

THE LARGEST BUBBLE GUM BUBBLE EVER BLOWN WAS AS WIDE AS TWO BASKETBALLS!

MAJOR LEAGUE OUTFIELDER'S CHEWED GUM FETCHES $10,000

TUCSON, ARIZONA, U.S.A.

Why pay a wad of cash—$10,000 to be exact—for some chewed gum? It all started when Jason Gabbert, a sports memorabilia store owner, asked a ballpark security guard to pick up a wad of chewed gum that Arizona Diamondbacks outfielder Luis Gonzalez had discarded at a spring training game. Gabbert put the gum up for auction, but when a bidder questioned its authenticity, Gonzalez chewed another wad of bubble gum in front of TV cameras. Bidding for that gum shot up to $10,000. It was all for a good cause: The money went to a scholarship fund for a Minnesota high school.

THE HAIR OF FOOTBALL PLAYER TROY POLAMALU OF THE PITTSBURGH STEELERS IS INSURED FOR $1 MILLION. POLAMALU IS FAMOUS FOR HIS THREE-FOOT (1-m) -LONG LOCKS.

TENNIS STAR'S PONYTAIL DISPLAYED

NEW YORK CITY, NEW YORK, U.S.A.

Tennis star Andre Agassi was known for his cool image and his long, flowing hair. In reality, he wore a hairpiece for years to hide the fact that the top of his head was balding! When Agassi eventually decided to shave his head, he had his ponytail (which was his real hair) snipped off. He donated it to a Times Square sports bar, which put it in a display case on the wall along with other valuable memorabilia.

SUCH AN IMPRESSION ON SPORTS HISTORY THAT ONE FAN PAID $6,500 FOR HIS FALSE TEETH IN A 1999 AUCTION AT SOTHEBY'S IN NEW YORK.

THE NEED FOR SPEED

LES ARCS, FRANCE

NOPE, THAT'S NOT A SKIER ZIPPING DOWN THE MOUNTAIN RESORT of Les Arcs, France. It's a bike rider on snow! The former stunt double has made his own name for himself as a downhill biker. And at age 53, French daredevil Eric Barone shows no signs of slowing down. Nicknamed the "Red Baron," Barone, in 2012, flew down the icy French slope at 138 miles (222 km) an hour, setting the world record. No stranger to speed, the racer also holds the record for fastest bike ride on gravel. He set that record while whooshing 107 miles (172 km) an hour down the side of a volcano in Nicaragua! From ice to lava, the Red Baron gives new meaning to *extreme* sports.

Tennis balls are never where they're supposed to be, even at the International Grand Prix! Austria's Jürgen Melzer can attest to that.

[AWKWARD MOMENTS IN SPORTS]

The wide world of sports is filled with slipups and oops moments. The best athletes just get right back into the game. These tough players have given it their all, not always with the intended results.

The 2006 World Wrestling Championships in Budapest, Hungary, were head-over-heels fun.

A **WORLD RECORD** WAS SET **IN CHINA** WHEN **1,377 PEOPLE** EACH **JUGGLED** A SOCCER BALL WITH THEIR **LEGS, FEET,** AND **HEAD** AT THE SAME TIME FOR **10 SECONDS**.

Is this a wardrobe malfunction, or an attempt to keep warm? This British Columbia Lions defensive tackle is the only one who will know.

"CATCHING IT FAT" IS THE TERM USED WHEN A **GOLFER'S CLUB** HITS THE GROUND BEFORE MAKING CONTACT WITH **THE BALL.**

Fore! Maybe Darren Clarke wanted to take home some souvenir grass from the 2005 Irish Open golf tournament.

Heads up! The human face has 43 muscles. These Olympic athletes seem to be using all of them at once!

WHERE *VICTORY* SMELLS *LIKE...* CHEESE

GLOUCESTERSHIRE, ENGLAND

Each year, Coopers Hill in the village of Brockworth becomes host to a unique tradition—a cheese-rolling competition. Thousands of people flock to the annual spring event to watch eager (and hungry) competitors chase a large roll of Double Gloucester 656 feet (200 m) down the steep grassy hill. The cheese is usually the hands-down winner, but the first *human* across the finish line gets to take home the cheesy prize.

No one knows for sure when the cheese games began, but they have been rolling at least since the 1800s. They've become so popular that one year they attracted 15,000 spectators, who jammed the quiet village to watch racers chase a Double Gloucester roll downhill at 70 miles (113 km) an hour.

For safety reasons, contestants now chase an eight-pound (3.6-kg) foam cylinder "cheese" instead. But the winners still get to take home the real cheese to chomp on. And you never know what these fun-loving competitors will do next. One winner has even raced in a ninja costume. Long live the cheese!

SOME **STINKY CHEESES** ARE **BANNED** ON **PUBLIC TRANSPORTATION** IN **FRANCE.**

FOLLOW THAT CHEESE!

A TRICKY TURN!

GOTCHA!

THE WORLD'S **MOST EXPENSIVE** CHEESE—MADE FROM **DONKEY MILK**— COSTS OVER **$500** A POUND.

ANIMAL
ATHLETES

SEA OTTER
SHOOTS HOOPS
TO HELP HIMSELF

SEA OTTERS
HAVE THE
THICKEST FUR
OF ANY ANIMAL—
1 MILLION HAIRS
PER SQUARE INCH!
(6.4 sq cm)

PORTLAND, OREGON, U.S.A.

Why is this sea otter playing basketball? Doctor's orders! Eddie is one of the older sea otters at the Oregon Zoo, and he needs to keep active. So his trainers taught him to flip a light ball toward a basket with his flippers. Eddie has since developed an excellent slam dunk, and his hoop dreams have helped improve his health, too. The exercise helps ease his arthritis, a stiffness in his joints. He may not compete on a sea otter team, but when it comes to practicing, Eddie's really on the ball!

NEWS FEED

>>> **MUMBAI, INDIA:** BATHERS AT A PUBLIC SWIMMING POOL IN A SUBURB OF MUMBAI WERE JOINED EACH MORNING FOR A WEEK IN THE SUMMER

THIS DOG'S GOT GAME!

THE AVERAGE DOG CAN LEARN 165 WORDS AND HAND SIGNALS.

DEL MAR, CALIFORNIA, U.S.A.

Think volleyball can be ruff stuff? Not if you're Petey the border collie! The dog scores big in the talent department. He not only plays volleyball—he plays better than most humans. When Petey and his owner successfully lobbed a volleyball 32 times in a row, the pup's antics went viral on the Internet. Like any well-trained athlete, Petey also plays it safe. He has booties to protect his paw pads on hard or hot pavement. He also uses a special volleyball that is soft on his mouth. This crackerjack canine even has his own YouTube channel. Now that's nothing to yap at.

IN ONE YEAR, A SHEEP GROWS ABOUT 8 POUNDS (3.6 KG) OF FLEECE!

COUNTING SHEEP

GREAT BIRCHAM, NORFOLK, ENGLAND

On your mark, get set, *baaa!!!* Among the many festivities held at Bircham Windmill's annual Country Day festival is sheep racing. While onlookers cheer them on, the woolly contestants—complete with stuffed "jockeys"—run a racecourse set up with hurdles. Although the flock may need to be coaxed with a bucket of feed to get the group bounding toward the finish line, the event ends up being sheep thrills for the whole community!

OF 2013 BY AN UNEXPECTED LAP-SWIMMING GUEST—A WILD MONKEY FROM A NEARBY GARDEN. TALK ABOUT MONKEY BUSINESS!

EARLY **TENNIS COURTS** WERE **HOURGLASS** SHAPED.

TENNIS BALLS' HAIRY ANCESTORS

1000

Life was tough before sporting-good stores. Early tennis players made balls out of wads of hair, wool, or cork. The balls were then covered with cloth or leather and tied up with string. Voilà! Tennis, anyone?

>>> SURPRISING SPORTS STORIES

1947

ROLL A STRIKE, PRESIDENT TRUMAN!

Even presidents need to have fun. A bowling alley was built in the West Wing of the White House as a birthday gift for President Harry S. Truman. In 1950 players on the White House Bowling League included members of the Secret Service, household staff, secretaries, switchboard operators, and groundskeepers. The alley closed in 1955, but two others were built later and used by bowlers-in-chief Presidents Johnson and Nixon.

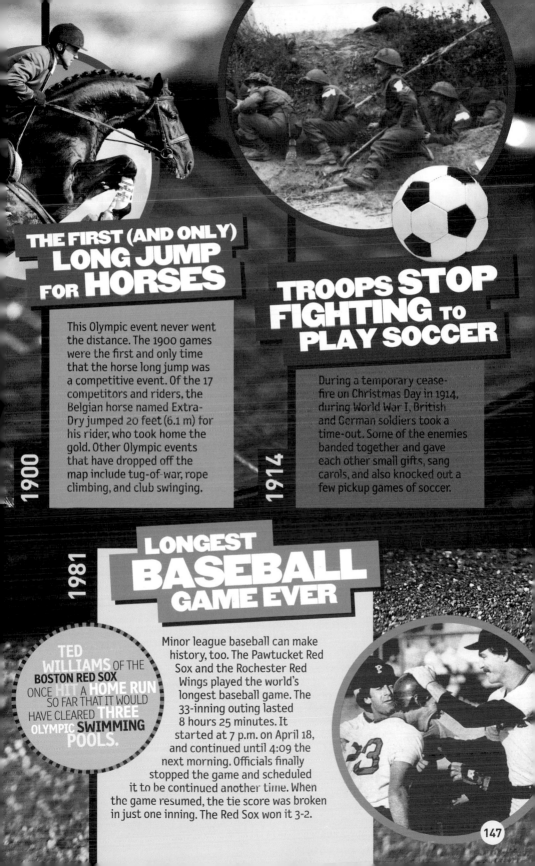

THE FIRST (AND ONLY) LONG JUMP FOR HORSES

1900

This Olympic event never went the distance. The 1900 games were the first and only time that the horse long jump was a competitive event. Of the 17 competitors and riders, the Belgian horse named Extra-Dry jumped 20 feet (6.1 m) for his rider, who took home the gold. Other Olympic events that have dropped off the map include tug-of-war, rope climbing, and club swinging.

TROOPS STOP FIGHTING TO PLAY SOCCER

1914

During a temporary cease-fire on Christmas Day in 1914, during World War I, British and German soldiers took a time-out. Some of the enemies banded together and gave each other small gifts, sang carols, and also knocked out a few pickup games of soccer.

LONGEST BASEBALL GAME EVER

1981

TED WILLIAMS OF THE BOSTON RED SOX ONCE HIT A HOME RUN SO FAR THAT IT WOULD HAVE CLEARED THREE OLYMPIC SWIMMING POOLS.

Minor league baseball can make history, too. The Pawtucket Red Sox and the Rochester Red Wings played the world's longest baseball game. The 33-inning outing lasted 8 hours 25 minutes. It started at 7 p.m. on April 18, and continued until 4:09 the next morning. Officials finally stopped the game and scheduled it to be continued another time. When the game resumed, the tie score was broken in just one inning. The Red Sox won it 3-2.

WACKY RECORDS
SHATTERED!

See how well you can identify each of these oddball sports records. Use the teaser clues to help you. Then impress your friends with your new knowledge! The answers are on the bottom of page 149.

COLLEGE STUDENTS IN CALIFORNIA PLAY THE WORLD'S LARGEST DODGEBALL GAME ON SEPTEMBER 24, 2011.

1. In 2011, how many people participated in the world's largest dodgeball game?
a. 4,488   **b.** 3,038,882   **c.** 203

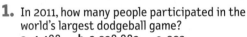

IN 2012 ROBERT MARCHAND COMPLETED A RECORD 300 LAPS IN 4 HOURS 17 MINUTES 27 SECONDS.

2. How old was the world's oldest centenarian cyclist to complete 62 miles (100 km) on a race track in Lyon, France?
a. 99   **b.** 100   **c.** 82

THE **WORLD'S**
LARGEST
WATERMELON
WEIGHED AS MUCH AS
A **ROTTWEILER.**

DAVIDE CENCIARELLI SHATTERED THE WATERMELONS, AND THE RECORD, ON JULY 12, 2012.

3. What is the greatest number of watermelons that anyone has ever smashed with bare hands in just 60 seconds?
a. 2   **b.** 70   **c.** 14,000

4. The world's longest tennis volley took 14 hours 31 minutes. How many thousands of consecutive strokes were in this exhausting record volley?
a. 2,594   **b.** 25,944   **c.** 2,594,044

OVER
50,000
TENNIS BALLS
ARE USED AT
WIMBLEDON
EACH YEAR.

5. In 2009 marathon runner "Bob the Carrot" set a world record for a marathon, but not for his running time of 3 hours 34 minutes 55 seconds. What record did Bob set?
a. Fastest runner eating food during the race
b. Tallest and thinnest runner in the race
c. Fastest runner in a vegetable costume

6. What's the record for the most people doing jumping jacks in a 24-hour period?
a. 17   **b.** 300,265   **c.** 10,000,000

CHAPTER 8

CULTURE SHOCK

YING PINBALL A CRIME • TEEN DESIGNER DRESSES
ORITE CHILDHOOD TOY • SUPER SOARING SUPER
DIANA JONES TAKE UP RESIDENCE • ROCKIN' UND
MENTS BUILT BRICK BY TINY BRICK • S
UND INSIDE WALL • W

SCENT OF A
SUPERHERO,
PAGE 161

T. REX CHASES WEDDING PARTY!

VIRAL ALERT!

BATON ROUGE, LOUISIANA, U.S.A.

In May 2013 a giant *T. Rex* chased a wedding party, and a photographer caught the frightening action. The catch? The photos were staged. Knowing that the groom loves dinosaurs, the photographer set up the shot with the wedding party and instructed them to "Run right at the camera, away from the *T. Rex*, as passionately as you can. I need to see fear and actual running, not lame faces and power walking." He later added the fierce dino into the picture. While the couple was on their honeymoon, the photo was posted online and it became an Internet sensation.

YODA AND INDIANA JONES TAKE UP RESIDENCE

WHO CLASSIC FILM STAR FAVORITES YODA (OF *STAR WARS* FAME) AND INDIANA JONES

WHAT BRONZE STATUES

WHERE IMAGINATION PARK, SAN ANSELMO, CALIFORNIA, U.S.A.

WHEN JUNE 2013

WHY WHO NEEDS STATUES OF TOWN FOUNDERS AND HISTORIC FIGURES WHEN YOU CAN HAVE YODA AND INDIANA JONES? GEORGE LUCAS, LONGTIME RESIDENT OF SAN ANSELMO AND CREATOR OF THE WIDELY POPULAR STAR WARS AND INDIANA JONES MOVIES, GAVE THE STATUES TO THE TOWN. THEY ARE A TRIBUTE TO THE PARK'S NAME—IMAGINATION.

NEWS FEED

>>> **NEW YORK CITY, NEW YORK, U.S.A.:** THE CITY'S OFFICIAL "FAMILY AMBASSADORS" WERE UNVEILED AS THE MUPPETS! MISS PIGGY, KERMIT, AND MORE

TEEN DESIGNER
DRESSES CELEBS

ENCINO, CALIFORNIA, U.S.A.

Most fashion designers only dream of designing for celebri-ties and hitting the big time. But by age 13, Cecilia Cassini had already done that, creating clothes for the likes of actress Sofia Vergara, model Heidi Klum, and singer Taylor Swift. Cecilia started designing when she was 3, and became mega-inspired at 6 when she got her first sewing machine. Now 15, she says she is so successful because she knows what girls love to wear, like feathers and bows!

WORLD'S LARGEST HOUSE OF CARDS

MACAU, CHINA

What does it take to make the world's largest freestanding house of playing cards? Exactly 218,792 cards. The replica of the Venetian hotel in Macau, China, was planned and assembled by Bryan Berg, an architect, inside the hotel in 44 days. Weighing more than 600 pounds (272 kg), the model was roughly 33 feet (10 m) by 10 feet (3 m), and no glue or tape was used to hold it together. That's over 4,000 decks of cards, in case you're counting!

POPPED UP ALL OVER THE BIG APPLE TO SHOW THAT IT'S A GREAT PLACE FOR "FAMILIES, FROGS, PIGS, BEARS, AND ANYONE ELSE TO VISIT."

ROCKIN'
UNDERWATER
CONCERT

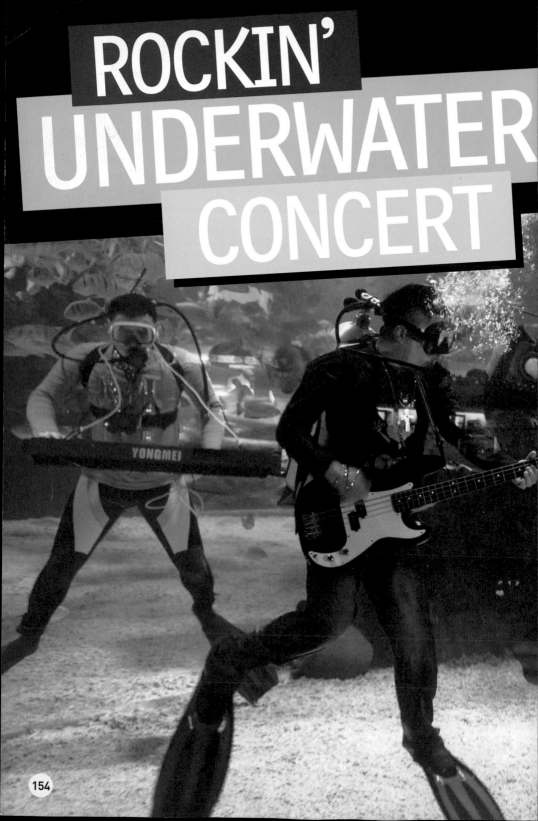

TIANJIN, CHINA

WHEN THE WATER'S YOUR STAGE, you can swim wherever your flippers take you! To make a splash about an upcoming festival, employees at Tianjin Haichang Polar Ocean World suited up in scuba gear, strapped themselves to musical instruments, and rocked out underwater at the aquarium. Prerecorded tunes allowed the musicians to focus on making the most of their moves with their guitars, drums, and electric keyboards. Rock on!

CANSTRUCTION IS AN ANNUAL **COMPETITION** WHERE PEOPLE MAKE **SCULPTURES** FROM **CANS** OF **FOOD.**

MOSS MUTT THIS PERKY PET COMPETED IN A SCULPTURE CONTEST HELD AT THE MONTREAL BOTANIC GARDEN. THE SCULPTURES HAD TO BE MADE MOSTLY FROM PLANTS.

[TOTALLY WILD ART]

Artists are known for thinking outside the box. Check out these clever creations. They just might inspire you to start painting or sculpting—or whatever!

HOLY COW! DRESSED FOR OUTER SPACE, THIS FLOATING COW SCULPTURE MADE ITS DEBUT IN STOCKHOLM, SWEDEN.

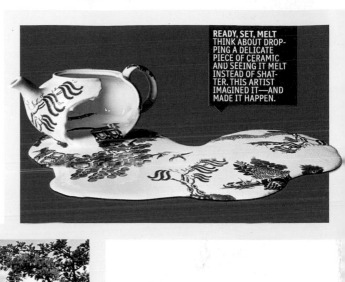

READY, SET, MELT THINK ABOUT DROPPING A DELICATE PIECE OF CERAMIC AND SEEING IT MELT INSTEAD OF SHATTER. THIS ARTIST IMAGINED IT—AND MADE IT HAPPEN.

THE WORLD'S HIGHEST ALTITUDE ART EXHIBIT WAS HELD IN AN AIRCRAFT AT 33,300 FEET.
(10,150 m)

TALENTED TREES CAN TREES DRAW? THEY CAN, AND DO, WHEN AN ARTIST ATTACHES DRAWING TOOLS TO THEM, THEN WATCHES WHAT HAPPENS WHEN THE WIND AND TREES INTERACT ON CANVAS.

ROLLING ALONG THIS TINY CUT-PAPER SCENE IS INSTALLED INSIDE A TOILET PAPER TUBE.

TWEETY TYPES THESE QUIRKY BIRDS ARE MADE FROM OLD TYPEWRITER PARTS.

LEGENDARY LANDMARKS, LEGO STYLE

MINI-MONUMENTS BUILT BRICK BY TINY BRICK

HONG KONG, CHINA

Some folks just follow the directions that come with the Lego box to put together a car or a ship, and that's great. But serious Lego builders take the colorful plastic bricks to a whole other level.

At the 2013 "Piece of Peace" exhibition in Hong Kong, Lego artists wowed the crowds with incredible re-creations of world landmarks, including St. Basil's Cathedral in Moscow, Russia, and the Sagrada Família church in Barcelona, Spain. Each display ranged from 800 to a whopping 100,000 pieces!

The "Piece of Peace" exhibition originated in 2003 in Tokyo, where Lego fans can view other landmarks, such as the Tokyo Tower, at the Legoland Discovery Center. Ready to start building?

ST. BASIL'S CATHEDRAL

SAGRADA FAMÍLIA CHURCH

THERE ARE
MORE THAN
915 MILLION
WAYS TO COMBINE
SIX LEGO
BRICKS.

THERE ARE
ABOUT
86 LEGO
BRICKS
FOR EVERY PERSON
ON EARTH.

TOKYO TOWER

SUPERHEROES
SAVE THE DAY

SUPER
SOARING
SUPERHEROES

SAN DIEGO, CALIFORNIA, U.S.A.

What if superheroes really could fly off to save the world? Well, they did, in San Diego, over Easter weekend in 2013. But they weren't quite the real thing. They were radio-controlled Styrofoam prototypes. Their designers, Otto Dieffenbach and Ed Hanley, sell the flying figures to advertisers, who can paint them to look like any superhero they wish, from Superman to Iron Man. Dieffenbach says he hopes the flying figures will also inspire kids to "build things for themselves and get away from just clicking a mouse."

IN THE FIRST **THREE YEARS** THAT HE APPEARED IN COMIC BOOKS, **SUPERMAN** COULDN'T **FLY—** HE COULD ONLY **LEAP** 1/8TH OF A MILE. (0.2 km)

NEWS FEED

>>> **ELKHART, INDIANA, U.S.A.:** ONE OF THE WORLD'S LARGEST SUPERHERO MEMORABILIA COLLECTIONS IS CONTAINED IN THE HALL OF HEROES, A MUSEUM

SCENT OF A SUPERHERO

LUTHERVILLE, MARYLAND, U.S.A.

If you could get up close and personal with your favorite Marvel comic book superheroes, what would they smell like? Now you can find out. Stan Lee's Signature Cologne was created to smell like he thinks they would smell—if they were real and wore fragrance, that is. The cologne is advertised as being "as adventurous as Stan's superheroes," yet "a bit villainous." Want to try a splash?

THE **HULK** WAS SAID TO WEIGH
1,040 POUNDS— (472 kg)
THAT'S AS MUCH AS A *POLAR BEAR!*

SUPER RARE COMIC BOOK FOUND INSIDE WALL

ELBOW LAKE, MINNESOTA, U.S.A. >>>

In 2013 David Gonzalez bought an abandoned home for $10,000 and began renovating it. One day he found a comic in the walls. Not just any comic. It was the world's most valuable comic, the one in which Superman debuted. It was Action Comics Issue #1 from 1938! It sold for $175,000. Now that's buried treasure.

THAT STANDS IN FOUNDER ALLEN STEWART'S BACKYARD. IT CONTAINS OVER 10,000 SUPERHERO ARTIFACTS AND MORE THAN 55,000 SUPERHERO COMIC BOOKS.

WHAT A ZOO!

ANIMALS EXPLORE THEIR CREATIVE SIDE

SOME ZOOS **DRILL HOLES** IN **COCONUTS** AND PUT *CRICKETS* INSIDE TO ADD A CHALLENGE TO **FROGS** LOOKING FOR A MEAL.

THIS SMALL MADAGASCAR HEDGEHOG TENREC IS A FOUR-PAWED PAINTER.

WASHINGTON, D.C., U.S.A.

Put a blank canvas and some paints in front of a tenrec and what happens? If you're at the Smithsonian National Zoo in Washington, D.C., the answer is a display of art. As part of an enrichment program, the zoo has art classes—for its animals! Tenrecs, armadillos, monkeys, pandas, and toucans are just some of the animals that have tried their hand—or foot or wing or beak—at creating art. The idea is for the animals to express themselves and improve the quality of their zoo lives. The paintings are abstract, to say the least. Monkeys and pandas hold a paintbrush, while other animals create splatters of color by rolling around in their own paintings. Hey, whatever works!

A GOLDEN LION TAMARIN DISPLAYS ITS TECHNIQUE.

163

FLIPPER HIGH HEELS SPEND A DAY SCUBA DIVING, AND THEN GO OUT ON THE TOWN AT NIGHT—WITHOUT A CHANGE OF SHOES!

[JUST FOR KICKS]

How weird or wacky can a shoe be? You might be surprised. Check out these samples of some seriously strange footwear.

PLAYGROUND HEELS WHEN YOU "SLIDE" INTO THESE DESIGNER HEELS, YOU JUST MIGHT TEETER-TOTTER, TOO.

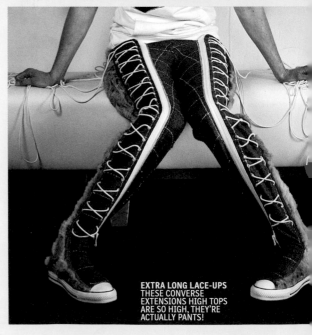

EXTRA LONG LACE-UPS THESE CONVERSE EXTENSIONS HIGH TOPS ARE SO HIGH, THEY'RE ACTUALLY PANTS!

BABY LACES FOR THE BABY FASHIONISTA, THESE FUNKY PUMPS ARE NOT MEANT FOR WALKING!

HEAVY-DUTY SHOES AT 323 POUNDS (146.5 KG) FOR THE PAIR, THESE SHOES ARE WORLD-RECORD BREAKERS. TAKE A STROLL IN THESE CLUNKERS.

YOU CAN BUY A PAIR OF **24-KARAT SHOELACES** FOR **$19,000.**

A MAN IN WASHINGTON STATE, U.S.A., OWNS **MORE THAN 1,500 PAIRS** OF **CONVERSE** SHOES.

TOUCAN HEELS WANT SHOES THAT REMIND YOU OF BIRDS? WELL, "TOUCAN" PLAY AT THIS GAME!

U.S. PRESIDENT INSPIRES FAVORITE CHILDHOOD TOY

1902

U.S. president Theodore (Teddy) Roosevelt was a famous big-game hunter as well as a politician. So when he refused to shoot a bear during a hunt, it made headlines. A newspaper artist drew a cartoon of him with a cuddly bear cub, and soon afterward stuffed toy bears became popular. They became known as teddy bears, in Roosevelt's honor. The rest is history.

PLAYING PINBALL A CRIME

1942

The seemingly innocent game of pongs, dings, and flashes known as pinball was banned in many American cities in 1942. Officials labeled it a form of gambling, saying it was a game of chance requiring no skill. The then mayor of New York City even signed an order allowing police to smash any pin-ball machine they found. The ban stayed in place in many cities until the mid-1970s. *Ding!*

>>> JUST PLAYING AROUND

IN 1952
MR. POTATO HEAD
BECAME THE FIRST **TOY ADVERTISED** ON **TV.**

G.I. JOE BATTLES BARBIE

1963

After Barbie dolls became a huge hit in the early 1960s, a competing toy company wanted to get in on the doll business—targeting boys instead of girls. G.I. Joe was invented in 1963 to give boys their own figure that could be dressed in different outfits and accessories. The loyal soldier has been deployed in the toy market ever since. Go, Joe!

CABBAGE PATCH KIDS CRAZE

1983

Parents knocked down displays and shoved their way in line to get their kids one of the strangest looking dolls in history. There was such demand for the dolls, advertised as "born in a cabbage patch," that many stores held lotteries for them. By buying a doll, you agreed to "adopt" it. By the end of 1983, some three million Cabbage Patch Kids "adoptions" took place across the U.S.A.

POTATO NOT INCLUDED

Hasbro's first Mr. Potato Head toy had no body! Kids had to supply their own real potato "body" to put the eyes, ears, nose, and mouth into. The inventor's first attempts to sell the toy, just after World War II, were not successful. Toy companies thought that parents would not want to waste good food for a make-your-own toy. But in 1952 the idea finally took off. Hasbro started selling the familiar toy with its plastic potato shape included in 1964.

TRENDING TIME LINE

Match these fads and fashion trends to the time when they were in style. The answers are on the bottom of page 169.

A. WIGS FOR MEN
After King Louis XIII of France started wearing a wig of long, flowing hair to cover his bald head, the trend caught on big-time with other men.

B. DANCE MARATHONS
Dance marathons were the ultimate test of endurance during the Great Depression. Some of them went on for weeks, or even a month. Contestants might get 15 minutes of rest each hour and some small snacks along the way. Gotta dance!

← **51 B.C.   1624   1900   1930**

C. DOG WALKERS
With so many people away from home during the day, who's going to walk the dog? Professional dog walkers! It's a *ruff* job, but these entrepreneurs have a howl of a time with it.

D. CLEOPATRA EYES
The ancient Egyptian teen queen—portrayed here by actress Elizabeth Taylor—led the trend of thick black eyeliner that extended past the eyes. The black goop reduced the glare of the hot desert sun.

E. CAR STUFFING
When the first Volkswagen Beetle came out, teens wondered how many people they could fit into it. Car stuffing became a craze. The standing record for stuffing is 20 people for the old-style Beetle and 25 for the new style.

1959   1960s   2014

F. MAJORLY MODEST BATHING SUITS
Beach bathers in this era didn't need to worry about whether they were showing too much skin—the bathing suit was a good excuse!

G. BELL-BOTTOMS
The funky fashionistas of the hippie era owe their bell-bottom styles to the U.S. Navy soldiers of the 1800s, who were the first to wear wide-legged pants.

CREDITS

Hera/Shutterstock; 84-85 (Background), NinaMalyna/Shutterstock; 84 (UP), CB2/ZOB/Supplied by WENN.com/Newscom; 84 (LO), CB2/ZOB/Supplied by WENN.com/Newscom; 85 (UP), withGod/Shutterstock; 85 (LE), CB2/ZOB/Supplied by WENN.com/Newscom; 85 (LO), CB2/ZOB/Supplied by WENN.com/Newscom; 86, Gero Breloer/picture-alliance/dpa/AP Images; 86 (LO), photastic/Shutterstock; 87 (UP), AP Photo/Bill Johnson; 87 (LO), Discovod/Alamy; 87 (CTR), photastic/Shutterstock

CHAPTER 5: Strange Science

88-89 (CTR), Piotr Naskrecki/Minden Pictures; 90 (LO), Gena73/Shutterstock; 90 (UP CTR), AP Photo/Isle of Wight County Press/Rex; 90 (UPLE), © Solent News/Splash News/Corbis; 91 (LO), © Erlie/Dreamstime; 91 (LOCTR), Associated Press; 91 (UP), AP Photo/Heng Sinith; 92-93, Martin Rietze/Westend61 GmbH/Newscom; 94 (UPLE), © Gerry Ellis/Minden Pictures/Corbis; 95 (LO), NASA; 95 (UP), Reuters/NASA/JPL/Space Science Institute/Handout; 96-97, CB2/ZOB/Supplied by WENN.com/Newscom; 97 (UP), CB2/ZOB/Supplied by WENN.com/Newscom; 98 (LO), © Mark Moffett/Minden Pictures/Corbis; 98 (UP), Rex USA/Sunshine Serpents/Rex; 99, Rex USA; 99 (LO), AP Photo/Ship to Shore Lobster Co., Elsie Mason; 99 (UP), © Phil Torres; 100-101, Michelle Soto M./La Nacion de Costa Rica/Newscom; 102-103, Mark Wilson/The Boston Globe via Getty Images; 104 (LO), © Heather Dewey Hagborg; 104 (UP), Chris Bott/ZUMA Press/Newscom; 105 (LF), Image Source/Getty Images; 105 (LORT), © Marcin Kubiak/Dreamstime; 105, AFP Photo/Northeastern Federal University/Semyon Grigoryev; 106 (LE), Hank Morgan/Science Source; 106 (LOCTR), Scorpp/Shutterstock; 106 (LORT), STILLFX/Shutterstock; 107 (LO), Photobac/Shutterstock; 107 (UP), gosphotodesign/Shutterstock; 108 (LO), George Haller, ETH Zurich; 108 (UP), Sam Gangwer/ZUMA Press/Newscom; 109 (LO), © Rose-Lynn Fisher; 109 (LO), © Rose-Lynn Fisher; 109 (CTR), ©Ammit/Dreamstime; 109 (RT CTR), AGCuesta/Shutterstock; 109 (UP), National Geographic Creative

CHAPTER 6: Way-Out Travel

111, © Anthony Redpath/Corbis; 112, Reuters/Mark Greenberg-Virgin Galactic/Handout; 113 (LO), Mars One/EyePress EPN/Newscom; 113 (UP), AP Photo/Bigelow Aerospace; 114-115, © Everett Collection Inc/Alamy; 116 (LORT), Kevork Djansezian/Getty Images; 116 (UPLE), © Grethe Børsum; 117 (CTR), Caters News Agency Ltd; 117 (LORT), Caters News Agency Ltd; 117 (UP), Andy

Trowbridge/naturepl.com; 118 (CTR LE), © John Iovine; 118 (LORT), © Think Geek; 118 (UP), CB2/ZOB WENN Photos/Newscom; 119 (LORT), Rex USA/Solent News/Rex; 119 (UP), Rex USA/Rex; 120-121, © Jake Warga/Corbis; 122 (UP), © Elizabeth Ruiz/epa/Corbis; 123 (LO), Juan Mabromata/AFP/Getty Images; 123 (UP), Michel Renaudeau/ZUMA Press/Newscom; 124-125, Sean Pavone/Shutterstock; 124 (CTR LE), AP Photo/Ahn Young-Joon; 124 (LOLE), © Anthony Redpath/Corbis; 125 (CTR LE), Junko Kimura/Getty Images; 125 (LOCTR), Yoshikazu Tsuno/AFP/Newscom; 125 (LORT), Yoshikazu Tsuno AFP/Getty Images; 125 (UPRT), © Photo Japan/Robert Harding World Imagery/Corbis; 126 (LOLE), © QEDimages/Alamy; 126 (LORT), Enrique R Aguirre Aves/Getty Images; 126 (UP), © imagebroker/Alamy; 127 (LO), Stefan Auth Image Broker/Newscom; 127 (UP), © Image Source/Getty Images; 128 (CTR LE), © Kerrick James/Corbis; 128 (LOLE), Jack Kurtz/ZUMA Press/Newscom; 128 (LORT), © dbimages/Alamy; 128 (UP CTR), AP Photo/Julien Behal/PA Wire; 129 (CTR LE), © Stéphane Lemaire/Hemis/Corbis; 129 (LO), Michael Durham/naturepl.com; 129 (RT CTR), Daisy Gilardini/Getty Images; 129 (UPRT), NGS Maps

CHAPTER 7: Weird World of Sports

131 (CTR), © Henry Browne/Action Images/ZUMA Press/Newscom; 132 (UP), © Jorma Luhta/Nature Picture Library; 132 (CTR), © Russell Cheyne/Reuters/Corbis; 132 (LOLE), © London News Pictures/Rex/Rex USA; 132 (LORT), © Bernd Thissen/Newscom; 133 (INSET), © Alexander Podshivalov/Dreamstime; 133 (UP), © Vaclav Volrab/Dreamstime; 133 (INSET), © Jules Frazier/Photodisc/PictureQuest; 133 (LO), © Melissa McCormack/AFP/Getty Images/Newscom; 134 (BACK), © Paul Hennessy/Polaris/Newscom; 134 (UP), © Wenn/Newscom; 135 (UP), © Gregg Pachkowski/ZUMA Press/Newscom; 135 (LO), © Remi Agency/ZUMA Press; 136 (CTR), © AP Photo/The Topps Company, Chip Litherland; 137 (UP), © AP Photo/Matt York; 137 (LOLE), © AP Photo/Bebeto Matthews; 137 (LORT), © AP Photo/Wally Santana; 138 (CTR), © Jean-Pierre Clatot/AFP/Getty Images; 140 (UP), © Dominic Ebenbichler/Reuters/Corbis; 140 (LO), © Szilard Koszticsak/epa/Corbis; 141 (UPLE), © Fred Greenslade/Reuters/Corbis; 141 (UPRT), © Toby Melville/Reuters/Corbis; 141 (LO), © Reuters/Corbis; 142 (CTR), © AP Photo/Tim Ireland/PA Wire; 143 (CTR RT), © AP Photo/Tim Ireland/PA Wire; 143 (LORT), © Rex Features via AP Images; 143 (UPRT), © AP Photo/Barry Batchelor/PA Wire; 144 (CTR), courtesy of Oregon Zoo; 145 (UP), © Jen Bergren/

Fetchlight Pet Lifestyle Photography; 145 (LO), © Albanpix Ltd/Rex USA; 146 (BACK), © Pearljamfan75/Dreamstime; 146 (LO), © AP Photo; 147 (UPLE), © pirita/Shutterstock; 147 (UPRT), © Hulton-Deutsch Collection/Corbis; 147 (LO), © AP Photo/Paul R. Benoit; 147 (INSET), © Jules Frazier/Photodisc/PictureQuest; 148 (UP), © Leonard Ortiz/The Orange County Register/ZUMA Press/Newscom; 148 (CTR), © Pascal Fayolle/SIPA/Newscom; 148 (LO), © Cultura RM/Alamy; 148 (UP), © Stephen Rudolph/Dreamstime; 149 (CTR), © Henry Browne/Action Images/ZUMA Press/Newscom; 149 (LO), Dan Westergren/NGS Staff

CHAPTER 8: Culture Shock

150 (CTR), © Jonathan Alcorn/ZUMA Press/Newscom; 152 (UP), © Quinn Miller; 152 (LO), © AP Photo/Marin Independent Journal, Alan Dep; 153 (UP), © Wenn/Newscom; 153 (CTR), © AP Photo/Kin Cheung; 153 (LO), © Reuters/Corbis; 154 (CTR), © Xinhua/Photoshot/Newscom; 156 (UP), © Mircea Costina/Alamy; 156 (LO), © John Lens/Alamy; 156, © John Lens/Alamy; 157 (UP), © Livia Marin, Nomad Patterns, 2012/Collection of Canterbury Museum, Christchurch; 157 (CTR), Tim Knowles; 157 (INSET), Tim Knowles; 157 (LORT), © Anastassia Elias/Solent News/Rex USA; 157 (LOLE), Jeremy Mayer; 158 (UP), © AFP PHOTO/Rie ISHIIRIE ISHII/AFP/Getty Images/Newscom; 158 (LO), © AFP PHOTO/Rie ISHIIRIE ISHII/AFP/Getty Images/Newscom; 159 (CTR), © Xinhua/Photoshot/Newscom; 160 (CTR), © Mike Blake/Reuters; 161 (UP), © Jonathan Alcorn/ZUMA Press/newscom; 161 (LO), courtesy of Comic Connect; 162 (CTR), Mehgan Murphy/Smithsonian's National Zoo; 163 (LO), Mehgan Murphy/Smithsonian's National Zoo; 164 (UP CTR), Paul Schietekat; 164 (LOLE), © Kobi Levi/Solent News/Re/Rex USA; 164 (LORT), Radek Leski/Studio Zupa; 165 (UPLE), © Facundo Arrizabalaga/Newscom; 165 (UPRT), © Photo by Heelarious/Solent News/Rex USA; 165 (LOLE), © Ivonne Wierink/Shutterstock; 165 (LOCTR), © Gordana Sermek/Shutterstock; 165 (LORT), © Kobi Levi/Solent News/Re/Rex USA; 166 (UP), © Bettmann/Corbis; 166 (LO), © David Hoare/Alamy; 167 (LE), © Reuters/Corbis; 167 (RT), ©Rex Features via AP Images; 168 (UPLE), © Bettmann/Corbis; 168 (UPRT), © Bettmann/Corbis; 168 (LO), © Tibor Bognar/Alamy; 169 (UPLE), © CinemaPhoto/Corbis; 169 (UPRT), © Bettmann/Corbis; 169 (LOLE), © Bettmann/Corbis; 169 (LORT), Wesley/Hulton Archive/Getty Images

PUBLISHED BY THE NATIONAL GEOGRAPHIC SOCIETY

Gary E. Knell, *President and Chief Executive Officer*
John M. Fahey, *Chairman of the Board*
Declan Moore, *Executive Vice President; President, Publishing and Travel*
Melina Gerosa Bellows, *Publisher and Chief Creative Officer, Books, Kids, and Family*

PREPARED BY THE BOOK DIVISION

Hector Sierra, *Senior Vice President and General Manager*
Nancy Laties Feresten, *Senior Vice President, Kids Publishing and Media*
Jennifer Emmett, *Vice President, Editorial Director, Kids Books*
Eva Absher-Schantz, *Design Director, Kids Publishing and Media*
Jay Sumner, *Director of Photography, Kids Publishing*
R. Gary Colbert, *Production Director*
Jennifer A. Thornton, *Director of Managing Editorial*

STAFF FOR THIS BOOK

Robin Terry Brown, Marfé Ferguson Delano, Becky Baines, Susan Bishanksy, *Project Editors*
James Hiscott, Jr., *Art Director/Designer*
Jay Sumner, Kelley Miller, Lisa Jewell, *Senior Photo Editors*
Rachel Hamm Plett, Dawn McFadin, *Designers*
Ariane Szu-Tu, Paige Towler, *Editorial Assistants*
Callie Broaddus, *Design Production Assistant*
Margaret Leist, *Photo Assistant*
Carl Mehler, *Director of Maps*
Deidre Hester, Andrea Menotti, Kathy Furgang, *Contributing Writers*
Julie Beer, Michelle Harris, *Researchers*
Grace Hill, *Associate Managing Editor*
Michael O'Connor, *Production Editor*
Lewis R. Bassford, *Production Manager*
Susan Borke, *Legal and Business Affairs*

PRODUCTION SERVICES

Phillip L. Schlosser, *Senior Vice President*
Chris Brown, *Vice President, NG Book Manufacturing*
George Bounelis, *Senior Production Manager*
Nicole Elliott, *Director of Production*
Rachel Faulise, *Manager*
Robert L. Barr, *Manager*

For more information, please visit nationalgeographic.com, call 1-800-NGS LINE (647-5463), or write to the following address:

National Geographic Society
1145 17th Street N.W.
Washington, D.C. 20036-4688 U.S.A.

Visit us online at nationalgeographic.com/books

For librarians and teachers: ngchildrensbooks.org

More for kids from National Geographic: kids.nationalgeographic.com

For information about special discounts for bulk purchases, please contact National Geographic Books Special Sales: ngspecsales@ngs.org

For rights or permissions inquiries, please contact National Geographic Books Subsidiary Rights: ngbookrights@ngs.org

Paperback ISBN: 978-1-4263-1514-5
Reinforced library binding ISBN: 978-1-4263-1515-2

Printed in the United States of America
14/QGT-CML/1